I WILL FIND MY WAY

COLLEEN DAVIS

This book is dedicated to:

Kelly and Lukas for the support they never even knew they were providing me. I am your biggest fan!

My Mom, Diane and Dad, Frank for their unconditional love and guidance. Thank you for all your sacrifices.

The additional two who made up the "Three Camino Amigos" Helene and Gōran. Thank you for seeing something in me that I thought had been lost forever.

And, to the rest of the Camino family I met along the way. We all shared in something way bigger than ourselves and I thank you for being a part of this wild journey with me.

Buen Camino!

INTRODUCTION

From Author's Camino Journal Notes

April, 2019 Entry

On Friday, January 11, 2019 at 10:00 pm something incredible happened. In a blink of an eye, I lost all grasp of logic, reasoning and total understanding of what was happening right in front of me. I was instantly swept up by a force of impenetrable armor that wrapped itself around my entire body allowing absolutely nothing to seep in. Although completely blind to all comprehension, I could still see what was occurring right before my eyes. It was just all happening in slow motion. I saw my fifty-seven-year-old husband, Garry, go into what I thought was a Grand mal seizure. I witnessed the nurses hook him back up to the monitors that were recording his heart functions. I heard them call the code blue and, in hearing that, stood cemented in place while what seemed like dozens of people ran past me, hands flaring all around me, grabbing for one thing or another. Slowly moving my head to the right, I could see my daughter-in-law with her hands over her mouth, staring back at me. The shock in her eyes was intense and telling. Hearing the words "crash cart", I found myself magically, and instantly, transported out of my husband's room and placed in the Emergency Department's hallway where reality finally broke through my daze and I immediately went into a full-blown panic attack.

My husband had gone into cardiac arrest after suffering a heart attack. He survived and is now "fixed" thanks to the talented doctors and nurses, the two stents in his heart and enough medication to cure just about anything. It's been 3 months (as I journal this) that this incredible turn of events happened and, although he has since had subsequent overnight stays in hospital and his heart continues to "flutter" several times a week, he is doing okay. Back to work full time, weekends are spent working on the car we are building together and the only difference in his life is that he has finally quit smoking and has lost some weight. Good things can come out of bad times.

Our next appointment will be on May 3, where we will hear the results of his echocardiogram and the twenty-four hour monitor he has had to wear due to the latest episode, but whatever the results are, I am still leaving for France on May 20 to walk the 810 km (or 500 miles) Camino Frances from St. Jean-Pied-de-Port to Santiago de Compostela, Spain.

Equipped with a backpack, a sentimental water bottle and a very special walking stick, I'm about to venture into the unknown. Welcome to this girl's very scary and exciting leap of faith.

PROLOGUE:

So, what brought me to that fateful day back in August 2018? The day I first heard about the Camino Frances and, subsequently, the day I decided to research it and, eventually take a forty day leave of absence from my job and my life, fly over the Atlantic Ocean and literally walk my way across Northern Spain – alone. Simple.... to find myself. Yes, that may sound a little corny but it was seriously that simple. To find myself. I had become so lost that I decided I was going to place myself as far away as possible with the intent of finding myself. Far away from outside influences, family, friends, work, noise, computers, responsibilities, routines, drama and distractions just so that the only voice I would hear was my own.

March 21, 2014, I was in a serious car accident. The authorities called it a "high speed rollover." I can't believe it has been that long. Time truly does fly by.

Prior to that epic and life changing day, I was working a full-time job in the travel industry. I was a Tour Coordinator for a motorcoach company. I had been at that particular company for four years at the time of the accident and, during that time, had been lucky enough to have had the opportunity to tour direct many wonderful tours that took me to some pretty cool places. When I wasn't tour directing the trips, I was in the office selling them. And, because that part of the job was commission based, it just meant that when the phone rang, I answered it. It didn't matter if it was 7:00 pm on a Wednesday night or 10:00 am on a Sunday morning.

At the time of the accident, I was also a newlywed. I met Garry on July 3, 2010, and we were married July 27, 2013. We met in a very interesting way. He drove past me one day as I was walking down the street and, because he liked the way my butt looked in my Lululemon's, he pulled his 55 Chevy Bel-Air over and asked me if I wanted a ride home. I knew him as a friend of my dad's and had remembered my mom describing the car before, so I really didn't see it as jumping into a vehicle with a total stranger. Plus, it was a 55 Chevy Bel-Air. Who can say no to that? To this day, I still don't understand how he knew where I lived but, I made it home safe and sound.

On the day before the accident, I was mad at him for some reason and had decided that I was going to jump in my car and drive down to Vancouver to see my adult child, Kelly, for the weekend. Although we had only been married for eight months, we had been together for three years and there were definitely things he could do to upset me. I may not remember the reason I was mad but I do remember playing this one specific song on my iPod Shuffle over and over again during my drive down. *Say Something* by A Great Big World. I belted out those lyrics until my throat hurt. Songs can be so therapeutic when you need them to be.

I hadn't told him I was going but I started feeling guilty so I gave him a quick call and advised him that I had left and wouldn't be back for a few days. I received a quick phone call from my Office Manager and, during a bit of a rest stop, I called my sister to let her know where I was and in less than an hour my life changed forever.

CHAPTER ZERO:
May, 2022 - Three years after walking the Camino Frances

As you may have already clued in, I kept a daily journal throughout my Camino and will be using those words, and others, as we work our way through this book or whatever it turns out to be. And, even though I have changed the names of some of the people I met along "the Way," it was only because I had no way of reaching them for permission to use their real names. Changing the names doesn't change the relevance of the roles they played along my personal journey.

My main objective, or goal, moving forward with this project is to try and connect with someone who is either thinking about walking a Camino, has walked a Camino or has maybe even walked several. Even better, I would love to just connect with that one person who has experienced or is currently experiencing some of the same issues that life has dealt me. Someone who has questioned or doubted the same things I have. Someone who has suffered and survived or maybe is currently still working it out. For me to see this as a success, I want to know that someone other than myself has read these words and goes away truly believing that they are not alone. To know that their thoughts and feelings are right and normal and sometimes even spot on. That no matter what they are going through, there is someone else out there who is going through the same thing and that they care. I have gone through those same things and I care.

I have experienced a lot of shit in my life. From an alcoholic parent to childhood sexual abuse; being mentally and physically abused by a significant other to having suicidal thoughts. I have been married three times, given birth once to a wonderful human being that I am proud to call my child. I no longer use the word "son" because they identify as non-binary and that's cool with me. I couldn't be prouder of them. I have moved around and moved on from a lot of different experiences. I have done a lot, seen a lot and experienced a lot and have no regrets in the process. I don't want to be a "Debbie Downer" and I don't believe I have ever been one. I have seen dark places but, thankfully, my resilience and stubbornness are extremely strong. Like most members of my family, I have a sick sense of humour that has helped me through some pretty terrible situations.

Anything that came up while transcribing my journal I have placed in italics. Whether it's helpful tips on the Camino, a bit of a back story, helpful words that you just may need to read right now or just me doing a little bit of venting – *they will all be in italics.*

If you actually think about it and have done the research on Caminos – we are all, really, living our own Camino. I believe that most of us are constantly looking for something and that we have, at one point in our lives, asked the question "Why?" or have uttered the words, "I just feel like I have lost myself." or "I don't even know who I am anymore."

People walk a Camino for all sorts of reasons. Historically, pilgrims walked the Camino for religious reasons, but now others walk to get back to nature, to disconnect, to reflect. They walk for the social aspect of it or to challenge themselves physically. I believe that most people who walk the Camino are walking it "to find something" or, if they aren't walking it for that reason, they probably end up finding something along the way. I definitely needed to find something and that one day back in August 2018, I decided that what I needed to find was in Northern Spain and that I was going to find it by walking across it.

And so, the journal, and journey, begins.

CHAPTER ONE:
May 19, 2019

I'm really not too sure what compelled me to pick up this journal and start writing in it back in April. And not only back then, but tonight as well. It has always been my intention to actually start writing in it tomorrow after I left home. Although I have journaled most of my life, I'm not even too sure what I want to come of this particular one. Will this just be a very detailed and therapeutic journal intended solely for my own use or do I want it to be something more? Perhaps share it with others who might find it of interest or, maybe, even connect with and go "Hey, she's writing about me, that is so my life!" Maybe I will just go with the flow and have it be what it will be. Just like they say about the Camino. Don't go in with any expectations – it will provide.

"How many more sleeps?" A question we always ask each other before one of us goes away on a holiday. This time the question is being asked of me from my sister, my mother and my grandmother. "Are you getting excited?" is another popular one. Well, I'm not. Is that strange? I still have so much more to do at work and so much stuff to take care of at home before I leave. Even though I am taking a leave of absence from my life, I still have to make sure that everything goes smoothly while I am gone. Strange concept, huh? But those aren't the reasons why I am not getting excited. I am the reason I am not getting excited.

For the last two weeks I have been second guessing my decision to go. I totally get that it is nerves, fear of the unknown and, definitely, doubts about my physical and mental ability to do this. But I have also been allowing all the things that other people have said to find their way into my head. "You know you are going to be lonely." "You can always quit at any time and go off and explore Europe." "Are you sure this is really something you want to do?" Well not anymore!

This has been the first major decision I have made for myself in a very long time. From the moment my car was forced off the road doing 110 km per hour to the split-second decision to swerve back onto the highway instead of hitting a cement post at 110 km per hour, that was really the last major decision I have made for myself in about four years. And that may be a little dramatic and a tad farfetched but, boy, does it ever feel that way.

You really can't understand it until you have been through it, and it doesn't necessarily have to be a motor vehicle accident. It can be any situation where you feel like you have, or have had to, hand your entire being over to someone else, or in my case, a whole lot of someone else's. Doctors, lawyers, physiotherapists, ICBC adjusters, other people's lawyers, chiropractors, specialists, more specialists, surgeons, occupational therapists and psychologists.

When I wasn't being pulled in one direction, I was being pulled in another. So, yes, I am having doubts because I am not used to this at all. Nobody is telling me or instructing me to do this. This isn't someone else's plan, agenda or instructions. There are no appointments being made for me or meetings to attend. This is all me and I am just not used to it. This is one hundred percent my decision.

I am also having doubts because, thanks to the accident, I now have PTSD and anxiety, so I'm afraid of just about everything. There are six planes and several trains involved in this adventure, as well as just over 800 km of "the unknown" I am going to attempt to walk – alone.

A little explanation regarding my PTSD and anxiety. I say "my" because, of the millions of people who have been or will be diagnosed with this mental health issue, their, or your, symptoms may vary. My hobby is drag racing. Kind of ironic considering that not only was I in this serious car accident, but I have also lost a very dear friend in a drag racing accident. I would like to think that this is a testament to my determination, resolve and strength to embrace life and to get back on that bike when I fall off.

So, as a drag racer, I go straight and fast down a drag strip and the analogy I use is this; "my" anxiety can go from zero to one hundred miles per hour in two seconds. It can literally go from, "everything is good and right in the world" to "total devastation and destruction," in a blink of an eye. It also has no reason, no logic, no filter and when it gets totally out of control, you might as well just stop trying to make me feel better and just let me hyperventilate until I pass out.

Other times, it's as if there is a major earthquake inside my body. And while my body is doing its thing, my mind could be telling me that my seat on the plane heading to France is going to be abnormally small, I will be surrounded by hundreds of people and we are all going to be so close together that I won't be able to breathe. This will cause me to freak out to the point that they are just going to throw me out of the plane in midflight. I am going to miss a connecting train and be stuck in a little village where no one speaks, or won't speak, English, I have lost my phone and have no way of communicating with the outside world or I am going to take a wrong turn on the Camino, my GPS, for some reason, is no longer working, I will have a huge panic attack, pass out and fall off a cliff. There is no such thing as logic when it comes to this condition and I know that it doesn't make sense, but that doesn't make it less real for me when I am going through it. The plane isn't going to crash and if I miss a train, oh well, I can probably catch another one. I am just afraid of the unknown. Bottom line. And, I believe that is normal.

What tells me that I am doing the right thing is that I have one day of work left and I am not freaking out about it. The thought of turning off the computer and putting it away for six weeks makes me feel like I am unlocking shackles. What tells me that I am doing the right thing is that I am going to be away from my husband for six weeks and it doesn't make me sad. What tells me that I am doing the right thing is that I'm not getting excited and that, to me, is not normal. I want to be excited. I used to get excited.

CHAPTER TWO:
May 20 and 21st, 2019 – Kelowna, BC to Paris, France

I have combined these first two days together because I started May 20 in Kelowna, British Columbia and by the time my connecting flight from Calgary, Alberta landed in Paris, France – it was May 21. I have included my route because no matter what Camino forum you go to, there is always going to be a question regarding how people actually found their way to the "starting line".

I am scared shitless. For the past two days I have been an emotional wreck. "Are you getting excited?" has been the obvious question asked whenever I run into someone, but it has been the hardest one to answer. I am sure somewhere in there is excitement but it seems to be buried underneath fear, doubt, anxiety and, did I mention – fear. It just doesn't seem real that in less than two hours I will be getting on a plane bigger than any plane I have ever flown in and it will be flying me to Paris, France. Like, really??

As I look around this building that holds all the International Gates, I am feeling like I don't belong here or I don't deserve to be here. It's like International flyers are a different breed all their own. They are all sophisticated, well dressed and walk with a sense of purpose while I am all redneck, carrying a backpack dressed like I'm about to hike in the woods for the next thirty-four days.

I remember feeling that way like it was yesterday. I had purchased some kind of energy bar and, after leaving the airport mini-mart, I immediately went looking for a place where I could hide out, eat my bar, read my rag magazine and just be left alone. It wasn't just the fact that I felt like I didn't fit into this whole International Flight Club, I had just really begun to distrust people. It wasn't something that happened overnight. I didn't wake up one morning, look around at my surroundings and decide that I no longer liked the human race. This was something that started to manifest long before that.

I have also been a bit overwhelmed by the amount of support and attention I have been receiving today. When you pack an item that looks like a sword wrapped in a homemade case, the airline staff and security team seem to show a lot of interest in it. It's a walking stick that my dad bought for me. He had spent several months trying to convince me that he either needed to go with me for support, advise me that I didn't really have to do this or, at times, explain how he felt I wouldn't physically be able to do this at all.

It is because of the stick and the airport staff's obsession with it that the story came out about me travelling overseas to walk the Camino. The airline check-in staff in Kelowna were very intrigued, amazed and supportive. One of them actually looked at me and said "Buen Camino." Apparently, that will be a phrase I will say and hear several times during the walk itself but it is a statement only those who have done a Camino would know to say. Another airline member allowed me to check the stick in free of charge when I was told by Security that it couldn't go on the plane with me. I would have paid double, even triple, but nothing is going to stop me from walking the Camino without that stick.

To clarify who my "dad" is, I am talking about my step-dad, Frank. He and my mom have been married for thirty-two years so that earns him the right to tell me what he really thinks and how he really feels. My biological father has no rights when it comes to me or my life. He is the alcoholic parent I mentioned before whose only goal in life seems to be to make everyone else's life just as miserable as his own. It's really very sad and I choose to feel sorry for him rather than to hate him for many reasons. That's another book all on its own.

So back to Frank. Although he had said on several occasions what his thoughts were on my decision to walk the Camino Frances, it was when he came home with this walking stick that really made me feel like he was rooting for me. He had purchased this stick in Banff, Alberta, especially for me and especially for my journey. It's a beautifully carved wooden walking stick with hand carved native designs and a slight sunken area that fits my hand like a glove. There is also a compass set into the top of the stick that clicks every time the stick itself touches the ground. I don't believe that compass ever really worked properly. For some reason, the stick was made in two pieces and screwed together, but when you looked at it, it had the appearance of a sword placed in its sheath. Hence the reason for airport Security's constant curiosity.

Another item that I would value, cherish and go through a crowded security check twice for in Madrid was a gift my child, Kelly, had bought me for Christmas. It was a green stainless-steel water bottle. Green has always been their favorite color and I have since adopted it as my own as well. I remember it was after receiving that water bottle that I finally sat down at the computer and purchased my plane tickets. I ended up dropping the water bottle on the first day of my Camino and now it has a permanent dent as a reminder of its own personal journey.

The decision to either bring a walking stick or two walking poles is definitely a preferred personal one and that's if you even want to bring any at all. If you are used to walking with two walking poles then take those; however, you will need to find out from your airline of choice whether or not you will need to check them or if they can go on the plane with you. I was told in advance that I would be able to take my walking stick on the plane with me but when I got to the airport and they saw that it was more than just a "cane", I had to check it as oversized luggage. Many people who walk a Camino are doing it on a budget so they choose to bring all their items from home; however, you may think about purchasing these items when you arrive in France or Spain, wherever your starting point is. There are many places that sell both walking sticks and poles.

My first flight was from Kelowna, BC to Calgary, AB. Fate sat me next to a single woman and we found ourselves in a conversation that lasted almost the entirety of that short flight. We discussed how we were both on a plane that was leading us to a new life and new beginnings. We talked about the fear we were both feeling because of the brave decision we had both made to get on this particular flight. But, as much as fear can be an uncomfortable feeling to experience, I have to sit in this fear and let it do its thing. I have to believe that I do deserve to be here and that I need this. I have to put down all my distractions so that I can clearly see, embrace and appreciate this journey. Fear is not going to stop me. It's making me sick to my stomach right now, but it is not going to stop me.

I have a feeling that this journal is going to be a roller coaster ride of emotions. I want to be as honest and "real" as possible because, although these feelings are mine and solely based on my life, it could truly be any one of ours. I married young, had a child, got a divorce (twice), had traumatic things happen to me and then one day I woke up and I didn't recognize the person looking back at me. All I saw were the labels I represent - someone's Mom, someone's Wife, Workaholic, Car Accident Victim, Codependent, Enabler – the list goes on and on. And although your trauma could be different than mine, the divorce count could be one instead of two or the list of labels could be different – it doesn't matter – my story is no different than a lot of others out there. Someone out there will relate.

I am also the type of person who lives their life doing for others. The person who people can rely on, come to and ask favors of because they know that I can't or have a very hard time saying "No."

So, when I say that I look around this International Gate area at the Calgary Airport thinking I don't belong here or that I don't fit in here, it's really because I have no idea where I belong or where I fit in. This journey that I am about to embark on normally doesn't happen to me because I am usually the one in the background making it possible for others to be able to do it. I create these adventures, I plan them, organize them and sometimes even pay for them, but I have never done anything like this for myself before because that would be – ready for it – "selfish". Well, is there anything wrong with that?

Day One turns into Day Two as I have now lost nine hours flying over the Atlantic Ocean and into France. With every little accomplishment, the fear is starting to fade. I have to say that the flight didn't feel as long as I thought it would. After takeoff, we were given a really nice meal which is something I am not used to on any flight I have taken. Chicken stroganoff, a small salad, a bun and a piece of cheese. That is more food than I usually eat in a day, especially these days. I must have slept through most of the flight because when I woke up, they were just about to serve breakfast, which was weird because it felt like we had just eaten dinner. I guess that's what happens when you lose nine hours while your eyes are closed.

After getting my luggage and walking stick, I went directly to where you buy tickets for the RER (Paris' rapid transit system), which was conveniently located inside the airport. I made it out of Charles de Gaulle, maneuvered my way around RER as well as the Paris Metro and, very easily, found my hotel. Then, after checking in, I ventured out to go see the Notre Dame (After the big fire. It was still beautiful but pretty sad to see the damage). I can not believe that I am writing down that I visited the Notre Dame in Paris. I also can't believe that I have actually accomplished all the things I have accomplished already. I am still very nervous about tomorrow as it is another day of travel. As much as I am still very afraid of the unknown, I feel that the farther away I get from my life back home and the closer I get to my adventure, the more at peace I am becoming.

On a side note, I do have to say that I think I have packed way too much as I am feeling very unorganized and bulky. I have a feeling I will soon be lightening the load - metaphorically, spiritually and literally.

As much as I want to include "instructional" notes about the Camino itself, every part of the Camino is a personal thing – from making that decision to walk a Camino to arriving back home having completed one. Some people make the decision to go and then jump on a plane the next day with basically the clothes on their backs and then others are like me. I researched the hell out of my Camino. There is a lot of very helpful and informative information on the internet including Camino forums and YouTube. I know this because I visited about ninety percent of them.

Whatever way you decide to approach and execute your Camino is the right way and don't let anyone tell you otherwise.

My decision to walk the Camino was made on a beautiful summer day in August 2018. A friend of mine had come by to drop a vehicle off at our house and, because he would need a ride back to his place, a mutual acquaintance arrived in a separate car. This person and I had had a falling out a couple of years prior but, for some reason, I felt compelled to approach her vehicle and throw out an olive branch as a way of ending whatever it was we were doing. She started telling me about her Camino and all I remember thinking was "Wow, this makes sense." Not only did it make sense; it resonated with me as something that I needed, and I literally mean needed, to do. So, I researched everything I could possibly research about the Camino Frances until the day I left nine months later. I chose that particular Camino because it was the most popular one and my reasoning was that there would be way too many other people walking it for me to get lost along the way. I figured I would just follow everyone else.

I also chose to hire a company to pre-book all of my rooms while I was on the Camino. I was in charge of booking my flights, my train to Saint-Jean-Pied-de-Port and my hotels in Paris pre and post Camino. Hiring a company to handle the rest allowed me to wake up each morning with one purpose for the day, to walk. Because the Camino Frances is one of the most popular routes and because everyone who walks it seems to follow the same guidebook, the experience can start to feel like a "bed race". You spend more time on your cell phone trying to book a room or speed walking to your next destination that you don't get to enjoy and take in all the beauty and history around you. Without having a confirmed place to lay your head at the end of a 32 km day, you are taking the chance that there may not be one available when you finally decide to stop. Especially in the more popular cities or towns. That only means you have to continue walking until you find a bed. "Bed Racing".

I had this company do most of the work for me because booking accommodations is what I do for a living and I really had no desire to try and find thirty-three different accommodations in thirty-three different places. I also went this route because I was mentally drained and there were literally days where even deciding what socks to wear sent me into a panic attack.

So, this just meant that my Camino had a pretty structured itinerary. It meant that I had to get up each morning and make my way to the chosen and pre-booked accommodation one way or the other. I didn't have the flexibility of staying an extra day in one of the bigger cities if I wanted to or I couldn't shorten or extend the number of miles I walked per day. The company I hired actually had planned for "free days" along the way but I chose to take them out and add them to the beginning and the end. In hindsight, I think I would have preferred to keep their chosen rest days as well, but I felt I didn't have the luxury of time.

I also decided to have my main bag transferred each day. I carried a daypack with me, which was still between eleven and twelve pounds depending on what I was packing, but my main bag would meet me at my next destination. The reason I chose to do the luggage transfer was because of the injuries I had sustained in the car accident. I had suffered neck, back and hip injuries and I wanted to make this journey as easy on my body as possible.

The revelation that hit me on that beautiful day in August and told me I needed to walk this Camino was because I had stopped feeling, if that makes any sense. And I had stopped caring. Although I had a husband and family around me, I found that I had detached myself from them all; except one. My nephew's little boy. And all those "things" I used to enjoy were no longer enjoyable so I threw myself into work. I had my job and I had my nephew's son.

I actually had a bit of a nervous breakdown about a week prior to my departure. I can't remember what made it happen, but I finally snapped. My husband just stood there and watched me. I can't remember him offering any kind of support, which shouldn't have come as a surprise because he isn't the type of man who gives much emotional support. He is a man's man who believes that if he goes out to the shop and builds me something, it will make everything better. It's really very weird and yet fascinating all at the same time. That breakdown was not just about him but he was definitely the one that night to tip the scale. It was also about the many expectations and obligations that had been placed on me, the accusatory and mean things said to and about me, the pile of responsibilities, whether mine or ones simply handed to me and the many hard to explain reasons and on and on and on.

My unhealthy attachment to work was to escape my everyday life. I would get up in the morning and start my work day as early as 6:00 am and then work straight through to 7:00 pm. And this wasn't just during the week. I did this on weekends as well. In a six-month period, I had actually banked enough overtime hours (meaning after my regular eight-hour day) to pay for four and a half weeks of my six weeks leave of absence.

Lukas, my nephew's son, was the reason my heart was still beating. He was four-years-old at the time and still pretty much non-

verbal, which was exactly what I needed. We really didn't need the words to make sense, we had our own way of communicating with each other. He gave me so much joy, love and laughter and what made it perfect was that there was no agenda. He didn't want or expect anything from me other than my time. There were no alternative motives, no drama, no backstabbing, no judgements. Lukas was my life line and work was my distraction.

The rest of my time (what little left I had) was spent researching every last detail of my Camino. I felt I had left no detail unresearched. The only thing I decided not to check out prior to my departure were the accommodations that had been chosen for me. All I had asked for was 1 to 2-star accommodations and I literally would have chosen 0 to 1-star if that had been an option. Just a room with my own bed and my own bathroom. I wouldn't know what type of room I had until I walked in the door. This was my Camino and that was the way I chose to do it.

CHAPTER 3
May 22, 2019 – Paris to Saint-Jean-Pied-de-Port, France

I can't believe I am on a train in France, staring out the window, unbelieving that I actually made all of this happen.

While researching this trip, I chose a hotel that was in the Montparnasse District of Paris. Not because it was close to the airport, but because it wasn't. I took the RER from Paris-Charles de Gaulle to one of its metro lines close to my hotel. I stayed in the Montparnasse District because it was in walking distance to the Gare Montparnasse – the train station and my next mode of transportation.

One of the questions I had asked on the Camino forum, and have since seen other people ask as well, was "If I am having my bags transferred each day, should I pack a suitcase or a backpack?" Again, that is one hundred percent a personal decision to make. I had convinced myself that I was going to be in a bad episode of Sesame Street – you know the one that asks, "Which one of these things just doesn't belong?" I figured everyone around me would be carrying everything they own on their backs while I dragged my suitcase behind me. That was not to be the case. Maybe in the very beginning, but not for very long.

I had purchased a hiking backpack online and, although it was awesome, it was just way too big for me. It included a daypack that zipped on and off and my original plan was to have the large backpack transferred and just use the daypack during the day but I found that even just putting the backpack on was bothering my neck and shoulders. What I ended up doing was just taking the daypack and a piece of carry-on luggage. The only time the luggage became a bit of a hassle was when my lodging wasn't equipped with an elevator or when I had to wheel it around on uneven surfaces, which Paris was full of.

Another piece of unsolicited advice is that if you are planning on walking the Camino, and you are travelling a fair distance to do it, I highly recommend staying an extra day in Paris, Madrid or any of the many cities involved in your pre-Camino travels. There was a nine-hour time difference (I was nine-hours ahead of my family back in Canada) and I had my first taste of jet-lag that would last for quite a few days. That extra day may be needed to get your bearings before embarking on your long walk.

While walking from my hotel to the train station, I came around a corner and stepped into this huge roundabout. Up until then, most of the buildings had blocked any type of "cityscape" views, but the area needed for this roundabout forced all the buildings to take a step back and I found myself standing face to face with the Eiffel Tower. Now, before leaving on this journey I had said that I would have to make a point of visiting the Eiffel Tower on my return trip to Paris because "I guess that's what you have to do when you are in Paris," but after seeing it this morning at a distance, I instantly got rid of that "poo poo" attitude and decided that I seriously need to go see it on my return. It looks amazing!

Although I know that I am physically here, I just keep telling myself that there are certain things that make this seem just a little bit more real. How can you not believe you are in Paris when, on your way to a train station, you just happen to run into the Eiffel Tower? It is real and surreal all at the same time.

I was wide awake at 3:00 am this morning and am currently on the train from Paris to Bayonne, then I will catch a smaller train from Bayonne to Saint-Jean-Pied-de-Port. Did I mention that I have never been on a train before? It feels like we are travelling at two hundred miles per hour as I look out the window and see green pastures, brick bridges and old farm houses all whiz by me. My emotions are all over the map and I just thought, after today, my only mode of transportation will be my own two feet (hopefully).

I started the day feeling a little panicky. Having never been on a train before only means that I have never been in a train station before either. So, when I arrived at the train station, I just naturally assumed that the first thing I would see was a train. That wasn't the case at all. It was like walking into a huge shopping mall. Well, a mall where every sign or written word was in a language I couldn't read, speak or understand. The people were friendly enough and they really tried their best to help, but it was still very overwhelming. I eventually found out that I was in the totally wrong building and that you don't actually see the trains in this station until you are standing right in front of them because they are all tucked away in their own individual little underground tunnels.

Holy crap the coffee on this train is strong! If I keep drinking this stuff, I will be running the Camino and I won't need any sleep.

I am a Tim Hortons coffee drinker and actually never acquired a taste for the European style coffee throughout the entire trip. I eventually switched to Coke Zero and I normally don't drink sodas. It's really weird what your body starts craving during something as strenuous and demanding as the Camino.

As more and more people get on the train, I am noticing more backpacks, walking sticks and fanny packs. Yes, I said fanny packs. I wasn't going to bring one but I noticed a few comments in the various forums I read suggesting that it would be a good idea and it really was. I can keep my phone, a little bit of money and other things like chap stick and candy in it. Just items you grab for on a regular basis and don't want the hassle of taking off your backpack every time you want or need it.

Once in Bayonne, I had seven minutes to find my connecting train that would take me to Saint-Jean-Pied-de-Port. It was not a big station by any means; however, the directions I was given were wrong and I found myself out on the street instead of on a connecting train. I literally grabbed the first person who looked like they worked there and pointed to my ticket. Had I missed it, there would have been another one a few hours later, but I made it on board with enough time to find one of the last remaining seats and have a good look around before the train started moving. Every single person on board was a pilgrim, fellow travellers embarking on the same journey I was about to embark on. I am finally starting to feel like I belong.

For most of the ride I just sat and listened to other people's stories, experiences of past Caminos, how much of this Camino they plan on walking and what the weather is supposed to be like. Apparently, there had been a lot of rain up in the Pyrenees and one fellow warned me that we would be walking in waste deep waters for the first couple of days. It sounds like it will be a great way to test out the rain gear I purchased at Value Village.

We finally arrived in Saint-Jean-Pied-de-Port and, immediately, I found myself following everyone else. I know now that a few of the pilgrims on this last train have done this Camino before so I followed them quite willingly. As we made our way up a small embankment, I got a glimpse of my first accommodation, the Hotel Central. I know from listening in on a few conversations that everyone was heading straight to the Pilgrim's Office so I decided that, considering I was the only one dragging around a suitcase, I was going to go check in to my hotel and then meet the rest of my fellow pilgrims there.

As excited as I was to explore this beautiful village, I chose to head back to the Pilgrim's Office and wait for the doors to open. Sitting beside a young girl who looked just as nervous as me, it didn't take long for the two of us to start up a conversation. She is originally from Vietnam but has been travelling for the last four years. She says she has no idea why she decided to walk the Camino, will probably not walk the whole thing and is hoping that she will find some answers to some questions along the way. She told me that "It will then be time to go back home…. unless I find a husband." We chatted about how each of our Caminos will look like for us and, after telling her that I will be having my bags transferred and that I will have my own accommodations, she crowned me with the title of "Rich Girl." If she only knew what I had to go through to be afforded this luxury.

This girl, whose name was Kim, would become my source of amusement throughout our time together on the Camino. She would introduce me to others as either the "Rich Girl" or "Carol". "At least it starts with a C," she would say to me after getting my name wrong for the fifth time. I eventually started agreeing with her that "Carol" was, in fact, my name.

Although she had started the Camino alone, she was very social and would join several groups along the course of her time on the trail.

But she would always find her way back to me during times where I needed a pick me up or a laugh. And I never took that "Rich Girl" as an insult nor did it feel as if she was calling me out as a snob or anything. Most of the people I met on my journey were walking the Camino on a very strict budget and I was too. You don't need to spend a lot of money once you are actually there and, instead of purchasing the Pilgrim's meal every day, I would go to a supermercado and buy my food, snacks and beverages there. As a matter of fact, I had very few Pilgrim's meals.

And I don't even want to say that I was "lucky enough" to be able to afford luggage transfers and private accommodations because I had to be in a serious car accident to allow me that "luxury". It really wasn't so much of a luxury as it was a necessity. And, believe me, after the first three days on the Camino, there were a lot more people making use of the baggage transfers.

I have signed my name to the official Camino Registry, received all the documentation given to me at the Pilgrim's Office and have donated a few Euro for a scalloped Camino shell of my choosing. No more planes or trains and no more preparing or planning. All I have to do tomorrow morning is get up and start walking.

In order to receive your Compostela, or "Certificate of Completion" in Santiago de Compostela, you must have walked the last 110 km of the Camino Frances. So, from Sarria to Santiago de Compostela you cannot use any other form of transportation than your own two feet. You must also collect one stamp a day until the last 110 km where you then have to collect two stamps a day. You will receive a Pilgrim Passport and your first "sello" or stamp at the Pilgrim's Office in Saint-Jean-Pied-de-Port. You then collect the remainder of your stamps each day at churches, bars or cafés and the albergues or hostels that you over night in.

I had joined the Canadian Company of Pilgrims and, for a small fee, received a Pilgrim Passport along with a patch that I sewed on to my daypack. You will need this Passport to show as proof that you are, in fact, a pilgrim at your various albergues and hostels. It is also what you will need to show to receive discounts on entrance fees to churches, museums and other attractions you may wish to peruse.

Saint-Jean-Pied-de-Port literally means "Saint John at the foot of the mountain pass," and is not only the starting point of the Camino Frances but is where three Camino paths meet. The Frances, Le Puy and the Vezelay. For me, it is the start of my own personal journey to find myself and, in order to do that, I have to be prepared. So, I ventured off to find the path itself just to make sure that tomorrow morning I will be heading in the right direction. It was a good thing that I did because I seriously would have gone in the wrong direction right from the start.

I also made the fair-sized climb to the site of an old medieval castle and its Citadelle on the top of Mendiguren Hill. I strolled around its moss-covered fortress walls that still seem to stand so strong and impenetrable. The area was also supposed to give me a great view of the Pyrenees but I am from British Columbia, Canada and we have the mighty and rugged Rocky Mountains so I am not really too sure if what I was looking at this afternoon is actually the Pyrenees and, if it is, then I am not too intimidated and have renewed faith that tomorrow won't be as bad as everyone has warned me it will be.

Those were the Pyrenees I was looking at and, I was very wrong in my assumption that they weren't going to be that hard to climb.

I also took some time today to call a few of my family members. I may want to shut out the world right now but I am not totally heartless. They have to at least know that I have made it here safe and sound. But after today, my cell phone use will be very limited.

I wanted to "unplug" as much as possible so I didn't purchase an international phone plan or a European SIM card. I had heard that the WiFi was really good on the Camino and the online guidebook I was given by the company I hired could be accessed offline as well. I consciously made the decision that if I wasn't using the free WiFi, then I just wasn't going online and, if I got lost on the way, then I was asking for directions.

I believe the first call I made was to my sister. It seems like she is always my first call. And, even though I felt that there were some issues that, one day, may need to be talked about, we are twins. She is the second half of me and she is the one I will always call.

She was my first phone call right after my accident. It was a clear Friday afternoon. Again, I was heading down to Vancouver to visit Kelly for the weekend. Just before Hope, BC, a pick-up truck passed me on my left but, before completing the pass, he started re-entering my lane. He eventually ran me off the road and, again, instead of crashing head on into a cement pole, I swerved back onto the highway, lost control of the car and rolled it down an embankment. Even though I hit my head on the driver side door, I did not lose consciousness so was witness to the dirt, debris, branches and car parts flying around outside of the vehicle as well as the various articles being strewn about inside. Shock had pretty much set in from the time I realized I was not going to stop in time to avoid going off the road to the moment the vehicle made its final resting pose on its passenger side. I must have touched the brakes at some point because the pictures I have seen clearly show skid marks but I don't remember. And I don't remember hearing the sound of the brakes, the impact or, really, the sound of anything. There was a lot to look at; however, as everything was happening in slow motion. I clearly remember the coins from my console and my iPod Shuffle flying in front of me in slow motion with the outside debris as their backdrop. The last thing I remember actually hearing was the sound of my own voice when I realized I was not going to stay on the highway and was bracing myself for the crash. I said out loud, "Here we go." I was preparing myself for either being knocked out or dying and just hoping that it wasn't going to hurt. The next thing I actually heard was the constant blinking noise of my hazard lights. The sound was so loud. Once I got my bearings back, I found my phone and called my sister.

So, again, the accident was on a Friday afternoon. After being trapped in the vehicle for over an hour waiting for the jaws of life to rip the car's roof off, I was transported by ambulance to one hospital and then, eventually, to another. My whole family came together that day with phone calls of concern and well wishes – it was quite overwhelming. You know who you are and I hope you know how much it meant to me. After being released, I spent the night at my brothers and then Saturday morning Garry and I made the very painful trip home, without my car. Instead of taking me directly home, we made a stop at my sister's place. Most of my family was there so it just seemed logical for me to go to them instead of them, individually, coming to my house. By Sunday morning everything and everyone, except for me, went back to normal.

It was a call I made to someone that Sunday afternoon that would start the ball of hell rolling. One that would continue to roll for over four years. "Could you drive me to the doctor tomorrow morning? I guess I have to let him know what happened and have him check me out. I don't have a car anymore." The answer to that question was "No." And, there was no real reason other than they just didn't want to.

I can't believe I am actually here and that tomorrow I will start a walk that will take me right across Northern Spain. I have had a few people today ask me why I am doing this and, especially, why am I doing this alone. All I have really told them is "I need a break."

The morning I left for this adventure, I laid in bed with Garry and told him that there was a chance we would not survive this journey as a couple. That I may come home and decide I no longer want to be married to him. I haven't worn my wedding ring since the last time he lied to me. That was about two months ago and it was really about something so stupid. My theory on this is very simple. You lie, you get caught lying, you promise never to lie again but then you continue to lie which then causes cracks in the foundation of your marriage. The foundation of the marriage is trust. You have no trust; you have no marriage. Period. And the trust issue is just one of a few issues that he and I have been having. I have a lot to think about during this journey and it's not all just about him. I could say that it is about a bunch of different people, events, situations and on and on but in the end, it's really about me.

They say the Camino has three stages: The Physical Stage, which starts tomorrow, the Emotional Stage and, finally, the Spiritual Stage. All the planning, anticipation and preparation stops here. Tomorrow, the real journey begins.

CHAPTER 4
May 23, 2019: Saint-Jean-Pied-de-Port to Roncesvalles
(Crossing the Pyrenees) - 25 km.

Holy shit!

That's really all that needs to be said about walking over the Pyrenees today. One blister just started to form and one of my big toe nails is digging into the skin so those are a couple of things to watch.

Although I did a lot of research, especially about foot care, one thing I overlooked was that when buying your footwear, whether they are hiking boots or hiking sneakers, make sure to buy one size larger than what you normally wear. I wore Salomon Trail Runners which were amazing; however, I bought the size I normally wear and that became a real problem. Little did I know that my feet would widen, swell and do whatever else they were going to do because of the extensive amount of pressure I was putting on them. Luckily, I had also purchased a really good pair of hiking sandals that became my saving grace at times.

I started today at 7:12 am, skipped breakfast and not just because I have never really been a breakfast eater, but mostly because of nerves. Also, the idea of climbing a mountain on a full stomach just didn't really appeal to me.

There was literally no amount of training that I, personally, could have done that would have prepared me for what I accomplished today. Having a full-time job combined with working a major amount of overtime did not allow me the time needed to prepare for this day. I thought conquering a hill near my home every day for a month was enough, but I was only kidding myself. Today was brutal but still very rewarding. I mean, today I climbed a friggin mountain in the Province of Navarre in the Spanish Basque Country. Who would have thought?

I met a lot of people today but a few really stand out as we all worked our way over the Pyrenees. First, are a mother and son from Cambodia. I actually started the day with them and, not only did they wait for me, they helped when my walking stick broke. I was maybe ten minutes in when the screw holding the two pieces together finally decided to give way. Together, we took what little supplies we had to actually fix a walking stick, meaning bandages and tape, and we fixed it.

The mom, Eada, has a backpack that is almost the same size as she is and, no matter how steep the climb was, she kept on moving. It may have been slow moving, which was fine with me, but she very rarely stopped. She would say that it didn't matter how slow her pace was or how long it took her, as long as one foot was always in front of the other. I eventually lost sight of them because I was taking a lot more breaks than they were. There were literally times where I would walk thirty steps, stop to catch my breath, then barely walking another thirty steps before having to stop again.

The other person is John from New Jersey. He is, admittedly, not in very good shape and we found ourselves joking and laughing about both of our physical capabilities on the many breaks we took together. He has a larger stride than I do so I would lose him in the mix only to catch up with him down (or literally up) the road. We would sit in a meadow, catch our breath and take in some much-needed water. The views of the day were spectacular. I climbed from 200 meters above sea level to just above 1,400 meters during most of this 22 km day.

As much as I tried to take in every moment of this first, and very difficult day, all I could concentrate on was forcing my body to put one foot in front of the other. At one point I even turned on my phone's video to capture the moment with narration but it was like I couldn't even muster up enough energy to create sound anymore.

It is said that what goes up must come down so, once John and I had finally reached the summit, we took a few minutes to rejoice in our accomplishment, catch our breath and take a few pictures and then it was time to descend. It was a steep descent into Roncesvalles. We went from that breathtaking 1,400 meters above sea level to 900 meters in only 4 short km. I promise not to be this specific with the distance or levels but this was an amazing feat and well worth mentioning.

Another thing that made this day even more spectacular was the fact that there was no fog. In most of the YouTube videos I had watched of others taking on this strenuous task during the month of May, there was always fog. Shots of them hearing the cowbells but never seeing the cows themselves. Reaching the summit and not having clear skies to look out at. I had beautiful views throughout the entire day and although there were days when the wind blew and the rain poured, for the most part, the weather was on my side the entire trip.

It was also during this first day that the wrong sized shoe would come into play. With every step during that downhill descent my big toe would hit the end of the shoe itself and, even though I had made sure to clip my toenails before I left for France and I tried to "toughen up my feet" for a few months before my travels, my big toenail would almost immediately start causing me problems, get infected and eventually fall off a couple months after I got home.

I literally climbed a mountain today and tomorrow I will continue to walk down it. It took me nine hours to do but I did it and I am so proud of myself!

My lodging for the night is at the La Posada de Roncesvalles, a hostel that dates back to 1612. Even though it is a hostel, I have my own bed and my own bathroom. Because there are limited options for meals in Roncesvalles, I paid the €10 for the Pilgrim's meal and was one of at least eighty people sharing a meal in the common room tonight. I was introduced to fellow Canadians in the lobby as we waited for the doors to open and when they were, we all crammed in like cattle. The room had wooden picnic tables that held about ten people per table and they extended from one end of the long room to the other. I followed my fellow Canucks but just as I got to their table the last seat was taken so I became the first person to sit at the next one, meaning I ended up at the end of the table next to the wall with no escape route.

The remainder of my table filled up quickly and it didn't take me very long to realize that they were all together and they were all speaking French. They don't speak a lick of English and I don't speak French. Let's just say that there were a lot of uncomfortable nods and smiles throughout the entire meal.

The meal. Bread and soup had already been placed on the table. I am not a soup person so I passed on that but I did take a piece of bread that came with no butter and, for a moment, I regretted my decision to not have some soup as it may have softened up the block of cement I was trying so hard to consume. Next, we were given a choice between fish and BBQed chicken. Both options came with French fries and I immediately perked up. The fish was served with the head and eyeballs still attached and I was very aware of this because everyone sitting around me had ordered it and I could feel four sets of fish eyes staring right at me. The chicken, which I ordered, was horrible. A perfect match for the dry bread was a dry piece of chicken with a side of dry fries. My dinner mates, who still didn't speak a word of English, were no longer trying to include me in any pleasantries as I continued to try to scarf down the worst meal I had ever had. I sat there waiting for anyone else in the room to make some type of move towards the exit and that would be my opportunity to follow suit. Again, I was trapped in the far corner of a long picnic table filled with non-English-speaking pilgrims who were now avoiding all eye contact with me, I'm tired, sore, still totally overwhelmed with everything and then just as I am about to give up all hope, dessert comes in the form of a drumstick. An ice-cream drumstick. How random and, yet, very much welcomed. It was absolutely delicious and I would have paid any amount of money for a second one but out of the corner of my eye I saw someone heading for the door and I was out of there.

After dinner I did try to take a look around but I am just way too tired to appreciate my surroundings. I know at some point today I crossed the border between France and Spain but I couldn't say where. If there were any signs or markers, I totally missed them. I am currently laying in a bed in a 17th century building surrounded by a village that has literally evolved around the Camino de Santiago and my mind is just way too exhausted to connect the dots to it all. I just want to sleep.

Colleen Davis

CHAPTER 5
May 24, 2019: Roncesvalles to Zubiri - 22 kms

It took me just over six hours to get from Roncesvalles to Zubiri, arriving here at 1:30 pm. Yesterday was a brutal day. If you are thinking about doing the Camino Frances starting in St. Jean Pied de Port, be prepared for a very long and hard first day, unless you have climbed Mt. Everest, then it should be pretty easy.

I am on this Camino to think. To think about what I want in life both personally and professionally. I am also on this Camino to take a well needed break from both my personal life as well as my professional one which should make the thinking process a little bit easier. Well, I'm telling you right now, there has been no thinking so far on this journey. My one and only thought and goal when leaving home was making sure I got to the "starting line" without getting lost in Europe and now that I have done that, the last couple of days have literally been about physically putting one foot in front of the other and dealing with the pain that has crept its way throughout my entire body.

These last couple of days have also been about dealing with the elements. Yesterday was hot and I had dressed for more of a cloudy day. I was thankful for the clear skies because it allowed for better viewing of the extremely beautiful and breathtaking surroundings, but it got pretty hot halfway up the mountain making the climb a lot more difficult. Today, it has been mostly wet, rainy and windy which made the downhill descent rather challenging. Rocks, clay and small, steep paths aren't very fun to walk down when they are wet. And that's if you can even call them paths. The area looked more like the aftermath of a rockslide. Even though I was following behind several people, every step was a personal choice as to where you planted your feet because there was really no clear path down and everyone was just doing their best not to fall. I almost fell three times and I had a walking stick. I can't even imagine what it would be like for someone who doesn't have a stick or poles. I can really see how people can get badly hurt during these sections of the trail.

Throughout the day I would stop to admire something amazing, whether it was a statue, an old church or a monument erected for a fallen pilgrim. I walked through villages that were so quiet and desolate that you would think they had been totally abandoned. I'd hear the ringing of the bells before seeing the sheep, cows or horses attached to them. At times, I would have to stop and take a few steps back to allow a herd of long-haired sheep to pass by or I'd find myself sharing the road with a few skittish cows who, by now, should really be familiar with the likes of a pilgrim. But even though those moments put a smile on my face, I still feel somewhat unattached. Especially today because of how damp, muddy and windy it was. Today, I was just too busy concentrating on moving my body to even try considering the objective of thought.

This was also confirmed by a woman I shared part of the day with. She started her journey a little further into France, so she has been walking a lot longer than I have. Of course, when you first start walking with someone the main question asked is, "Why are you walking?" or "Why are you here?" Her story is somewhat similar to mine. She said she has hit a bit of a crossroads in her life and would like some guidance with what direction she should go in. She told me that the first week is all physical. Aw yes, the Physical Stage of the Camino. I know I read it several times while doing my research but I guess I just didn't want to believe that I was going to be slapped in the face with it the second I started walking. Maybe I was hoping the stages would be more organic, subtle or even ebb and flowing from one to the other and back again.

And they would be. Of course, the first part of this was definitely going to be physical, especially for someone like me who had never actually climbed a mountain two days in a row before. Once my body started acclimating itself to the physical environment I had thrown it into, I found I was able to allow the emotional and spiritual parts in. They too would come and go throughout my time on the trail. I would experience huge physical, mental, emotional and spiritual moments intertwining with one another several times during my Camino.

I am also still suffering from jet lag. I went to bed last night at 8:30 pm and found myself wide awake at 11:45 pm. After only one day on the Camino, I laid in bed, tossed and turned and tried to convince myself that I have made the biggest mistake of my life. All night long I questioned my decision to be here. "I should call it quits." "My body is so sore." "I have so many doubts." "How the hell can I get out of here?" Here, I don't even know where "here" is. This small little Basque community somewhere in the middle of the Pyrenees Mountains is as far away from home as I have ever been and now, I am trapped here. "Maybe I should bus it to the next town and then to the next and the next until this is all over." Lack of sleep, no appetite, aching big toe, aching body – the list goes on and on. And then just like that, it was morning. I got up, put on my gear and I walked most of the day in the rain and, for a brief moment I thought, "I can do this" and I did. With one foot in front of the other, I walked from Roncesvalles to Zubiri.

Finding my accommodation was really very easy considering it is literally the first Pension I saw when walking into Zubiri. The Pension

Zubiaren Etxea is a small bed and breakfast situated right next to the river. It has maybe four quaint private rooms and a small common breakfast area all located on the bottom floor of what, I assume, is someone's home. Immediately following check-in, I jumped in a well needed shower with all my clothes on. It was the easiest way I could see getting all the mud and dirt off my clothes so that I can start nice and fresh tomorrow morning.

I then went out to explore. You see, it doesn't matter how grueling the day has been, you still have to go out and enjoy the sights. I came across a sporting goods store and, because my daypack has been putting too much pressure on my shoulders, I bought a new one. This one has a specific spot for my water bottle and better padding in the shoulder straps. It also has a waste strap which will take a lot of the pressure off my shoulders. I guess my daypack was really quite old. There was no side compartment for my water bottle so I had to clip it to either my jacket or one of the bottom straps of the pack itself. So, the bottle has spent most of the last couple of days swinging back and forth with every stride I took, hitting whatever body part that got in its way. Now, it has a nice little home of its own.

I also ran into New Jersey John during my evening stroll. We shared a cocktail and some laughs with three fellow pilgrims before I made my way back to my room. The rebar enforced window of my room offers me a wonderful view of the river and the gothic bridge that crosses over it. It is currently rainy and windy which I hope will stop by morning. Now that I have this new pack, I will attempt to take my Camino patch off the old one and sew it to the new one. Good thing I packed a little sewing kit.

I don't know what tonight's sleep will be like. Will I toss and turn and try to talk myself out of this? Maybe. What I do know is that I will get up in the morning, put on my gear and start walking again.

CHAPTER 6
May 25, 2019: Zubiri to Pamplona - 22 kms

    This morning on the trail I decided to start talking to myself – out loud. "Right now, it is 1:00 am back home and look at me, I am walking across Spain!"

    I spent most of the day walking in solitude. I would see the same people off and on for the first part of it, but there came a time where all of a sudden everyone just seemed to disappear. I realized during my time alone just how much I enjoy the sight and sound of water. Following the Arga River for most of the day added to the peacefulness of those alone times. And I have to say that the medieval bridges I am crossing are absolutely breathtaking.

    Walking into Pamplona was like walking into a 15th century Roman Fortress and I guess it's because it kind of is. But to be perfectly honest, I am not a huge fan of Pamplona. I got lost as soon as I walked into the city itself and, on more than one occasion, I had to ask for directions. My offline guidebook comes with a GPS that is supposed to assist me in finding my hotel, but it seemed like it was just as lost as I was.

    The city actually has a "lift" or an elevator that takes you from one street up (or down) to another. I know this because I had to use one after getting lost for the second or third time. Plus, the streets are so confusing and narrow and full of crisscrosses that I was afraid to go out and explore in fear of never finding my way back to my hotel. I eventually braved my environment and went for a little walk, but basically tried to stay in a straight line to make sure all I had to do was turn around and walk that straight line back to my hotel.

I made it to the nearest café, bought a smoothie and struck up a conversation with a father and daughter from Australia. There are three children in his family and when he can, he likes to take each individual child on a vacation for a little bonding time. It might not always be to Spain, but this is where his daughter really wanted to go.

The "neighbourhood" I am staying in was having a block party today, so right from my window seat in the café I got to enjoy some music, people singing and playing instruments and every once in a while, a mini parade would pop up out of nowhere. The Spaniards really do know how to throw a party.

My accommodation tonight is the Hotel Eslava, which is located in one of the corners of Pamplona's Old Town. The reason I know it is in one of the corners of Old Town is because of the angle of the medieval wall enclosure I was walking on earlier right across from my hotel. Fortress, Citadel, Castle — it just boggles my mind that these have become so tangible to me.

My room is nice; however, the streets are narrower than what I am used to back home in Canada. I find this has been the case in all the hamlets, villages and cities I have been in or walked through. Back home, I live on acreage so I am used to open spaces, not crammed in places.

I had said in the beginning that this is going to be a time when no one else will tell me what to do and that all the choices made will be mine and mine alone. Well, this evening I decided I will not be walking tomorrow. It is not because I don't think I can do it because I know I can but I have looked at the elevation map from Pamplona to Puente la Reina and have read what the guidebook has described for tomorrow's path and it is very clear that there will be a very steep climb and an even steeper descent with slippery and stone ridden sections.

My big toe on my left foot is calling the shots and I have decided not to take the chance of causing it more discomfort. It continues to rub at the tip of my shoe and has now become infected. I think I would be fine with the uphill climb but the descent is what causes the most damage and, instead of powering through and risking my ability to complete the entire Camino, I will take tomorrow off and give my toe the break it desperately needs. On an average day, injuring my big toe would not be a big deal, but I am only on day three of a walk across Spain where my feet are my most important body part and I really need to take care of them.

Having said all that, I feel like shit. I feel like I "should" get up tomorrow morning and start walking. As much as I know I need to sit in this guilt, frustration and angst and let those feelings work themselves out, it just feels so uncomfortable. This is where I need to just let it go and realize that this is how my Camino is going to be. It's also what self-care looks like, which is something I am not used to bestowing upon myself. I am usually too busy taking care of everyone else's needs to even consider my own.

That's me. The one who looks after everyone else whether they asked for it or not. I believe that is called "co-dependent". I was told once that how you treat yourself emanates to others. They see you treating yourself like crap, or in my case, just totally ignoring myself and in turn, figure it's okay to treat you that way as well. Monkey see, monkey do.

I honestly never really knew how to look after myself or, even if I did, I just didn't. I would push the limit, ignoring all the signs that a rest was needed. I would deny myself the self-care I was craving and then eventually would just break down. My body would either physically or emotionally make that decision for me.

I broke my collarbone once in a dirt bike accident. I did the best I could to take it easy, but the bone didn't heal properly and I had to have it re-broken and pinned two years later. I spent six weeks at my mom's house because she knew if I didn't, I wouldn't look after myself. Same with my hip surgery after my car accident. I spent a couple of weeks at Mom's house because she knew that if I had stayed home, I would have overdone things. She also knew, as did I, that Garry wasn't going to be available to me or my needs. He works outside of the home so that part is understandable, but we both knew that even when he wasn't working, he could be unreliable. While I was away, he would come and visit for a few minutes here and there, but from my observation he either doesn't possess that instinctive caring gene or it is just too uncomfortable for him to show it. Again, "man's man" kind of thing.

A strange thing happened though during the four years after my car accident. People stopped believing me. It was a really weird phenomenon that, even to this day, I can't understand or explain. And not just random folks. I'm talking about people who have known and trusted me all of their lives. People extremely close to me as well as a family doctor I had been going to for twelve years.

You only have to look at the aftermath of what used to be my VW Beetle to know that something serious happened so, maybe that thought process came from the fact that I didn't arrive back home with a missing limb or huge contusions all over my body. I did have bruises and I was picking shards of glass out of my head for some time after, but there was really nothing that would instantly give anyone the impression that I had been injured in a horrible car crash. So, my question then is, "What was it about me that changed that day to make certain people feel that this horrible car accident instantly turned me into a liar?"

Nothing showed up on any of the x-rays or CT scans on that fateful day back in March, 2014; however, I knew there was something wrong. I know my body and I knew something wasn't right. After the car rolled, it came to rest on its passenger side, leaving me somewhat hanging by the seatbelt. I believe the hip injury happened right after I took my seatbelt off and fell from the driver's seat over to the passengers. My left leg must have stayed in place, causing my hip labrum to tear in three places. The pain was instant, severe and persistent. It didn't matter what position I tried to get into, I could not get rid of the pain. It didn't help that I was experiencing neck and back pain as well so the ambulance attendants didn't want me moving at all. I don't know about you but when I am in pain, I need to move, so being stuck in a VW Bug for over an hour in severe pain while being told not to move was just as torturous as the pain itself. There were other injuries that day but my hip and neck really stood out above the rest.

Once the roof was taken off the car and the attendants were able to get me on the backboard, I asked one of them to grab hold of my leg to help stabilize it. He did and immediately became my official "leg placer" for the rest of the day/evening. When it got too sore in one position, I would ask him to move it either up or down, from one side to the other, bent knee, straight leg, pillow under it, no pillow – he was so kind and patient. But again, nothing showed up on any of the scans that were performed and, come to think of it, when I was discharged from the Abbotsford Regional Hospital the attending doctor looked at me and asked me why I was limping. You can't make this stuff up folks.

I did make it to my family doctor that Monday after the accident, a family friend drove me down there, but it would be the last ride I asked for. My vehicle was declared a "write-off" which means it was unrepairable and I was left without a mode of transportation. Going through my insurance company to get paid out was a bit of a process and then there was the task of finding another vehicle and that all took time. So, if I needed to go somewhere I walked. I walked slowly and painfully but I walked. Yes, I became a martyr. I sucked it up, I paid the price with pain – but I refused to ask anybody for anything.

It was a slow progression. It became apparent that my doctor was an advocate as long as I was upbeat and happy or as long as he felt that he was right. The second I walked into his office feeling a little down and somewhat depressed or dejected or if certain test results proved him or his theory wrong, his attitude took a drastic turn.

During one of his initial examinations of my hip I had winced out in pain. He suggested that it may be a labral tear. Because the insurance company refused to pay for an MRI and because I refused to believe there was nothing wrong with my hip, I borrowed the money from my parents and paid for the MRI myself. The test results came back as a hip labral tear.

Now, between the time he had suggested the tear and the time I actually had the MRI, he had switched gears. My list of ailments caused by this accident was growing. Physically, it had always been about my neck and my hip but, because of the accident, I was also suffering emotionally. I wasn't sleeping or, when I would fall asleep, I was having horrible and vivid dreams of death. I was in constant fear of dying or being hit by a car and I was starting to suffer from anxiety and panic attacks. So, besides going to a chiropractor three days a week and a massage therapist twice a week, we were getting rid of massage therapy and adding physiotherapy, counselling and sleep aids. He was now focusing all his efforts on the emotional symptoms.

When the results of the MRI arrived on his desk, he literally did not believe them. I say again, you cannot make this stuff up. Because I was involved in a lawsuit, I gained full access to all of my medical records. Every report, statement and sentence my doctor had written in his file about me was at my fingertips. Although he had initially suggested a tear, in his written notes he was now disagreeing with an MRI report and stated, verbatim, "I refuse to believe it is a labral tear until I hear it directly from an orthopedic surgeon." Well, I repeated that sentence to the surgeon who would eventually perform my hip surgery and I remember him looking at me in total disbelief and asking, "Does your family doctor know how to read an MRI report?"

I noticed that my doctor would flip flop from believing either the physical pain or the emotional trauma, but never accepting both of them at the same time and I will remember this particular day for as long as I live. I had come in to extend my leave of absence from work and he questioned why I felt I couldn't return to my place of employment. I started explaining my reasoning but it was only when I mentioned how the severe whiplash was causing me great discomfort, headaches, neck and shoulder pain and how it prevented me from performing everyday activities and chores that I saw this man, my family doctor of twelve years, the one I had recommended to several of my family members and whom, up until that moment, I still had some respect and trust for, do something so unethical that to this day, I still entertain the thought of reporting his actions.

You see, my husband had been in a very serious motor-vehicle accident over twenty years prior to me meeting him and, as a result of that accident, he can no longer move his neck. He doesn't suffer any pain and has not allowed this to interfere or prevent him from doing anything, but that day, as I tried to explain to my doctor why I didn't feel ready to go back to work, he literally jumped out of his chair and started imitating my husband and his impairments, but in a very animated and disgusting way.

The visual – Picture a grown man holding on to his neck with both hands, twirling around the room, deliberately bumping into the door and walls of his office while making his neck as stiff as possible and exaggerating his attempts to look around the room.

The narrative – "But what about Garry?" "Garry can't move his neck; Garry is in a lot of pain." "Garry can't help you because he can't move his neck." "I saw Garry in the mall and he was like this." (As he twirls around his office bumping into walls).

He then went into a rant about how "soft" Canada is regarding whiplash and that, in other countries whiplash isn't even recognized as an injury and, because of that, people are returning to work quicker.

It took everything I had not to burst into tears and run out of his office. Instead, I discussed this with my counsellor and it was decided that I would write him a letter letting him know how that one episode had made me feel. I also explained, in great detail, how this car accident had affected every aspect of my life. In this letter, I stated that I valued his opinion and expertise but, lately, I felt like he was not taking me seriously; even pointing out some of the times he just flat out called me a liar (Especially the MRI findings and the chores I said I could no longer do at home).

I submitted the letter on a Friday so that he had the weekend to read it. During my appointment with him the following Monday, he "fired" me as his patient. It had only been seven months since the car accident, I was awaiting surgery for a labral tear, I had a list of ongoing appointments and treatments I was regularly attending, I was suffering from anxiety, panic attacks and PTSD and he tells me that, and I quote, "I am done with you and there is nothing more I can offer." He then told me he feels attacked by this letter and believes that I am trying to manipulate him BUT he will continue to supply me with drugs until I can find another physician. I refused that offer. Oh, and as a parting gift he says, "Even certain family members don't believe there is anything wrong with you." I left his office, went to my vehicle and cried. Not only did I cry, I contemplated driving my vehicle of off a cliff. Instead, I called my chiropractor and the reason I called her was because she believed me. She talked to down from my tears and my thoughts and told me that she would do whatever she could to help me and she did. She made a phone call to one of her physician friends and, in no time at all, I had another family doctor.

In hindsight I want to say that firing me was one of the best things he did for me in all those twelve years. I am a big believer that certain situations will either bring out the best or the worst in people and he was proof of that. Again, it didn't matter what I went into his office with, as long as I presented it with a smile on my face and an "upbeat" attitude, then all was right with the world. The times I went in there feeling blue, gloomy and hopeless were the same visits where he'd reprimand, "educate', question and treat me with a 'less than" attitude. Invoke his authority and that is not right. Too many doctors have this "holier than thou" attitude. I have experienced it myself and have seen it with some of the doctors who have treated my brother and, again, it is not right.

I was at my most vulnerable and, in my mind, he took advantage of that. He had stepped over the line with the MRI diagnosis, the rant about whiplash and the childish imitation of my husband. His treatment towards me was unethical and his comments were unprofessional.

At that time, I was crushed. He was basically confirming how I was already feeling - alone. A liar, a fake, not worthy of support or assistance. A joke. I mean, if your doctor is giving off those vibes then it must be true. I started feeling like maybe everyone else was right and that I should be doing this or doing that. But the pain kept stopping me. The emotional trauma kept reminding me. The physical pain was real, the trauma was real.

But again, in hindsight he was doing me a favor. I now have a wonderful doctor, a supportive and caring doctor. I have also learned to advocate. Not just for myself, but for others. I know firsthand how hard it is to advocate for yourself when you are suffering and it is unfair that you should even have to, but, don't ever stop advocating for yourself. You know your body.

One of the first promises a doctor makes is: "First, do no harm." Some just need to be reminded of that. Advocate!

CHAPTER 7
May 26, 2019: Pamplona to Puente la Reina – 21 km

I need to take back what I said earlier about not liking Pamplona, but first, I want to say a few things about what I am seeing along this journey I am taking.

I am seeing beauty in everything I look at. I won't even try and pretend to know the first thing about history and I really haven't made a conscious decision to look up the specific historical fact about these items, places and objects that I sometimes find myself standing right in front of. I do know enough to understand that the paths and roads I am, have, and will continue to be on (and I use the word roads very loosely at times) are Roman and ancient roads. The bridges I walk over and the statues I gaze upon are literally thousands of years old. The pictures I take are capturing items representing thousands of years of historical moments that have led to this particular juncture in time. That was a pretty deep sentence to digest and what's even more mind-blowing is that I have now become a small speck of that objects history just by standing in front of it. It really is quite overwhelming.

So, that part I wrote earlier about getting lost in Pamplona, well, that was just Pamplona doing its job. The Romans strategically built the city the way they did so that if and when their enemies penetrated the walls, they would get lost within the cities maze.

Okay, so taking back what I said about "not liking Pamplona". Because I made the decision not to walk this part of the Camino, I decided to give Pamplona another chance. Walking out of my hotel, I turned left rather than right this time and found myself strolling through a beautiful park with statues and nicely groomed foliage. I wandered down streets that were a lot wider than the ones I found myself trapped in last night and, because today is Sunday, nothing much was open and other than the occasional jogger, there were very few people on the streets.

While exploring the city, I did see some of my fellow pilgrims and the guilt started to creep in. I felt like a total failure considering I couldn't even make it four days without having to "cheat". I walked around the city for two hours and, even though I thoroughly enjoyed it, I kept telling myself that I probably "should" have sucked it up and just walked to Puente la Reina. I still feel that way but I need to let that go. I need to focus on the positive that came with my decision. I got to see some amazing sights, I have some beautiful pictures, I was able to light a candle for some friends back home who asked me to do just that and, more importantly, I would have left Pamplona with negative feelings about it had I not given it that second chance. So, after exploring the city, I packed my belongings, minus the articles I continue to leave behind, and took a taxi to Puente la Reina.

Having not walked this section of the Camino I did miss out on seeing the Pilgrim's Sculpture on the Alto del Perdon or Hill of Forgiveness. This was something I had seen on many YouTube channels and was really looking forward to seeing it in person. I was; however, reassured by several people who had, in fact, walked today that I had made the right decision. Apparently, due to the weather, the descent was extra treacherous. A slight concession.

Just to clarify the part where I say "minus the articles I continue to leave behind", it's not like I throw things away, toss aside or forget to pack. In almost every albergue, hostel and even at some hotels, you will find some type of box, drawer, cabinet or basket where pilgrims dispose of articles of clothing, bandages, sunscreen, lip balm or various other objects that another pilgrim may need. That particular day, I left behind a sports bra. Again, I did a lot of research on this and found that there were quite a few things I packed that really came in handy. Others, not so much. I joked that all I really needed to walk the Camino were my shoes, my walking stick and my water bottle but really, there were a lot of other things that were just as important.

Arriving mid-afternoon allowed me the opportunity to explore the medieval town of Puente la Reina. This is where the two main routes of the Camino Frances and the Camino Aragones converge. Getting lost a few times in both Pamplona and Puente la Reina has not only raised the number on my step counter but it has also led me to what is now my favorite place on the Camino.

Puente la Reina, the 11th century Romanesque bridge that gave its name to the town, literally means "Queen's Bridge". Simply put – it is stunning! Definitely something that needs to be seen in person because there are no pictures that give this masterpiece the justice it deserves. Because this bridge marks the beginning of my journey tomorrow, I won't walk over it until then. I did; however, end this emotional roller coaster of a day by sitting on the grass next to the River Arga admiring the bridges' amazing architecture and its seven semi-circular arches. I wasn't the only one. As I watched some of my fellow pilgrims walk into town and then eventually find their way to the grassy hill, I would smile at them with pride for their accomplishment of completing today's walk. I also felt a bit like a fraud for making the decision not to.

As I looked around and watched as pilgrims came and went, some staying only for a few minutes and others choosing to allow the bridge to become their backdrop for a picnic dinner, my mind started to wander. It has only been four days and, although I have run into many familiar faces and shared moments of pleasantries with many people, I know very little of them by name. Still, it is like we have already started becoming a family.

I sigh in relief when I see an older gentleman, who I know is walking alone, slowly make his way into town or I look forward to passing, or being passed by, a fellow pilgrim whom I recognize right from the train in Saint-Jean-Pied-de-Port and sharing a smile. It's like I have already started caring for these people, their wellbeing and their achievements. It will be interesting to find out just how many of them I will see at the square in Santiago de Compostela.

My accommodation is at the Hotel Rural El Cerco which is located right in the heart of the historical center. Unfortunately, the window in my room gives me a view of the property next door, especially the dog that has been chained up in his backyard all afternoon and now into the evening. I am a huge animal lover and my heart aches for this defenseless and lovely creature. The room itself is really quite small but very cute and, most importantly, has the two things I requested out of my accommodations, my own bed and my own bathroom.

Writing about the afternoon sitting by the Puente la Reina reminded me of a couple of important things to share. I had become more rigorous about my "training" approximately a month prior to leaving for Spain. It was during that training that I started getting pain in the arch of my right foot, which turned out to be plantar fasciitis caused by the repetitive strain I was putting on my foot. I ended up buying some orthotics for my shoes, which helped tremendously.

When I was at the bridge, I saw a lot of people stretching (as was I) and that is why I remembered this part. Shin splints. The inflammation of the muscles, tendons, and bone tissue around your tibia that causes pain. I started getting them on day three so I did some research and found a really good site that explained five very effective exercises to do for shin splints. I would do these exercises every morning before I began my day and then again every night.

CHAPTER 8
May 27, 2019: Puente la Reina to Estella – 22 km

I am so happy to be back on the Camino. Last night I finally broke down and took an Ativan to help me sleep. I tucked myself into bed and turned on an episode of *Border Security* which, to my surprise, was being aired in English. Two hours later, I woke up with the lights and TV still on and so confused that I literally had no idea where I was. It scared the crap out of me. Thanks to the Ativan, I had no problem falling back to sleep and actually didn't wake up until my alarm went off this morning.

Breakfast was a piece of toast with jam (again, no butter) and a freshly squeezed glass of orange juice. I took a couple of muffins for the road and off I went.

Today was filled with an eclectic cast of characters. I met Margaret from San Diego, Mark from San Francisco and I'm not really too sure where Scott is from but I have run into him enough times that we both recognize each other and are now on a first name basis.

Like a soap opera being played out in real time, Scott and Mark would eventually join up with a few others and become an inseparable gang. Together, they would rent apartments and hotel rooms to help with the cost. My comic relief buddy, Kim, would become a part of that clan for a while as well. Scott and Emily, a girl I walked with off and on, would eventually become a couple. Emily was from London and she had been travelling around Europe with her boyfriend. To finance this adventure, they would pet and house sit in various locations. Her beau had to return home so she decided to continue the Camino alone and then make her way back to London afterwards. We would spend a lot of time talking about our lives and what brought us both here. I found her adventures very interesting and thought, in a former life, that would have been me. Emily and Scott eventually "hooked up". I spent a lot of time listening to her explain her inner turmoil about spending time with someone else while still in a relationship with another. I'm not one to judge so I lent my ear, gave advice when it was asked for and basically allowed her to process and then proceed. I believe what she was looking for was approval, which was so unnecessary. This was her journey and, obviously, this was what her Camino was providing. And even though this group of people I found myself not only surrounded by, but actually diving into some heavy conversations with, were more my kid's age than mine, I felt it was all happening for a reason so I just went with the flow. They thought I was cool too.

I spent most of my day with Paul from Orlando and it was definitely MY Camino that brought the two of us together because I learned a lot from him. On several occasions I have told my husband that I feel he is never "there for me". For the most part I feel like he is emotionally unavailable to me, but I also feel I never really have his full attention and asking him to assist me with something is almost as painful as just doing the chore myself. Well, Paul's wife also suffers from chronic pain and feels like he is not there for her either.

It is really interesting to hear the "other side" from someone who represents the flip side of the coin, so to speak. And because I am not emotionally attached to this man, he said he found it easier to articulate what he needed to say to me opposed to trying to explain it to his wife. He told me he felt he WAS honestly trying to help and be there for his wife. That everything he did was an attempt to make her life better and, although he was struggling and suffering himself, he looked at me and said, "But it's just way worse for the person who is going through the illness – the one who actually needs the help." Huh, is it? I found myself sympathizing for him and, from what he was telling me, it sounds just as hard for the person trying to provide the help as the person who actually needs it. Not only was he trying "his best" to assist her or trying to do more for her; he was doing it all while feeling like he wasn't doing enough or being told that it wasn't enough. He was doing all this while also dealing with his own problems both in his personal life as well as at work. Things that he didn't share with his wife because he didn't want to burden her with them.

So, then I find myself questioning why it's possible for me to show this man who I have only spoken to for an afternoon more compassion and understanding than I can for Garry. Maybe because I am not emotionally attached to this man. Garry doesn't talk to me, especially about his feelings. Garry doesn't seem to listen to me, especially about my feelings.

Right after my accident, I was not given the opportunity to rid myself of any prior burdens or responsibilities and put all my time and energy into healing, both physically and emotionally. Instead, all my new issues just started piling on top of my old ones. What I did do though was keep the lines of communication, at least on my end, open. I told Garry what I needed. I was very straightforward with him, sometimes brutally straightforward but, then again, I learned right after the accident that I would have to become my own advocate. I also learned that, even though I was asking for help or advising him of my needs, he had stopped listening.

The way I see it is, if you truly love someone it should just come naturally to be there for them no matter what. In good times and bad, in sickness and health. Isn't that what we vowed to do? But, in speaking with Paul today, I have come to realize that maybe it is just a lot more complex than that.

The question I now need to ask myself is, "Do I want to delve into that complexity with Garry?" or do I just want to continue to believe that if you actually love someone it should just come naturally. When Garry is hurt or sick, I immediately ask what I can do to make his world a better place. It's like breathing, I don't even have to think about it. Is it so bad to want to believe that love works that way?

As for the trail itself, it was a beautiful day on the Camino. A seesaw kind of day with lots of hills, more up than down it seemed. It was along this stretch that I walked on a beautifully preserved section of a Roman road. Again, I am not well-versed in history but when all I have to do is look down and see that I am physically walking on the foundation of a road that the Romans once used and that history is literally at my feet, it's pretty overwhelming. I may actually be stepping in the exact same spot as one of the first pilgrims did while making their way to Santiago de Compostela to gaze upon, what they believed to be, the relics of St. James himself.

My accommodation in Estella is the Hotel Yerri, which is nice enough; however, it is on the outskirts of town and nowhere near the Municipal Hostel. Even if I wanted to spend some time with other people, after checking in, tending to my feet, showering, washing my clothes and strategically hanging them out the window to dry, I just don't feel like walking that far. Instead, I will opt for a snack at a nearby supermercado and a night in.

This would be the case at several of my stops. Because I pre-booked all my accommodations, I left it in the hands of the company I hired to choose them all. Next time, and there will be a next time, I will ask for accommodations that are either on or just off the Camino itself. As long as I have my own room and my own bathroom, it honestly does not matter what "star" rating the place has.

Before retiring for the evening, I messaged Kelly and was told that all of their friends think I am pretty "cool". Well, that part is true (ha ha), but Kelly also said that they are really proud of me and that hit me right in the heart. Those words will get me through any challenge I am currently facing or will face along this journey I am taking.

CHAPTER 9
May 28, 2019: Estella to Los Arcos – 21 km

Going to the bathroom while on the Camino. This was one of the conversations I had with fellow pilgrims today. In all the research and YouTube videos I watched, this topic was never addressed. I guess I was under the impression that, because the Camino Frances is the most popular Camino, an opportune time to answer nature's call would be hard to find. Believe me, there are plenty of opportunities to just drop your drawers right in the middle of the trail, do your business, and then keep on walking. I wouldn't suggest doing that. Maybe take a few steps off the path before doing your business, but the point is, I am not going to worry about that anymore. I have a bladder the size of a pea and have been consciously making a point not to have my café con leche until after my day is done, but not anymore. What I am finding is that I can drink as much as I want throughout the entire day and not have to go to the bathroom for hours. I guess it is just coming out as sweat instead. And, if I do find myself in the position where I can't hold it until the next stop, I find an appropriate place and let er' rip. Just like everyone else.

My day started at just before 8:00 am. I allowed myself that extra time because it was a rather short day today. The wind; however, was constant with just a bit of rain. The funny thing was, it didn't matter what direction I was going in, the wind seemed to be always hitting me in the face.

I had heard about the infamous Fountain of Irache or the "Wine Fountain" and figured, even though I am not a wine drinker, I would partake in a sip. Well, if there hadn't been a group of people standing by the closed iron gates, I would have walked right by it without even knowing what it was and, for just a second, I considered doing just that when I realized it would be another ten minutes before the gates opened up. But instead, I reminded myself that it is not just about the walk and that I need to take in every moment I am given on this Camino, so I waited. The novelty of this whole experience wore off the second the wine started trickling out of the tap at a snail's pace followed by the select few in front of me who decided they would fill their entire canisters and/or water bottles to the brim. I ended up filling a mouthful portion into my Camino shell and sipped out of that. The wine tasted terrible, but I was glad I waited and now have pictures to prove I was there.

Along with the constant wind and occasional drops of rain, today was another day of climbing. It was also the end to the more rugged terrain of the Pyrenees, hopefully. Leaving the gorgeous scenery of the Basque Country behind, I will start making my way through the La Rioja vineyards. Not far past the Fuente de Vino, the pilgrim is presented with a choice of two paths. The route to the left is a more direct route to Los Arcos and the route to the right is longer and has a steady uphill climb. Even though I was presented with more climbing, I chose to go to the right because it is the traditional way and it really wasn't as bad as I had anticipated. Reaching certain villages, I would look up on a lone hill to find the remains of a castle type structure; whether an actual castle, a monastery or maybe even a hospital, I am not sure. Needless to say, whenever there is a lone hill in a random village, there is likely to be that one structure perched high on it, looking down on us all.

One of the highlights of the day was the section where the two paths meet up again. There were no houses, no cafés, no real buildings at all but there sat, under a tree, an older woman playing the accordion.

When I arrived at this area there were already quite a few pilgrims who had gathered to take this in. And then out of nowhere, this group of Italians broke into song and a few people started laughing and then the laughter became contagious. It was just a wonderfully random experience shared by a bunch of strangers – or were we becoming a family?

Today was the first day that I actually used my earbuds in an attempt to listen to some music. I had downloaded a large collection of songs, a few podcasts and some audio books thinking I would need something to get me through some of the longer days; however, today has really been the first day I even thought about plugging in. And it wasn't so much that I felt like listening to anything. It was during a long 13 km stretch with no villages and the wind had been pretty consistent so I thought maybe it would be a nice distraction.

I also brought sunglasses that I hardly ever wore. It became a conscious decision right from the start of my Camino to see everything the way Mother Nature intended her hard work to be seen and I wanted to hear everything, even if it was just the sound of my feet on the path I was walking on.

After about five minutes of pressing play, I saw a group of people sitting on a grassy hill and decided I would rather do that instead so, I took off my pack and my earbuds and joined them. I spoke with some people I hadn't met before and then looked around and recognized a few others I have either passed or have been passed by. Kim walked by and shouting "Hi, Carol!" I corrected her this time.

Even though today was a rather short day (anything under 25 km is considered short), it felt a lot longer because of the wind that blew directly at me for almost five hours straight. The guidebook warned that there would be a long and monotonous 13 km stretch and even though there was, I was still able to find beauty, or at least serenity, in every step of this journey so far, even today.

Arriving in Los Argos, I met up with Paul and enjoyed a drink with him and his two Camino friends, Sara and Cameron. I know that Sara is walking alone, I just didn't catch a lot of her story; however, Cameron is from North Dakota and his husband will be meeting him to walk the last three days with him.

Before dinner, Cameron and I walked through the Church of Santa Maria. Needless to say, this was the first 12th century Romanesque/Gothic Church that I have ever stepped foot in and all I could say was "Wow!" It goes without saying that Cameron is more historically informed than I am so his reaction to the church itself was a bit different, but one thing we both agreed on is that there is definitely enough gold in that building to feed everyone in this town for at least one thousand years.

I am staying at the Casa de la Abuela, which means "Grandmother's House". Although it is an albergue, I do have my own separate bedroom and bathroom. The room beside me has eight bunk beds in it. I know this because Kim and her friends asked to poke their heads into the "Rich Girl's" room so I, in turned, asked to see what their room looked like. Well, this "Not so Rich Girl" is so glad she pre-booked all her rooms because first off, there is no way I would get any sleep sharing a room that size with seven other people and secondly, I ran into a few people this afternoon who have had to move on to the next town because everything in Los Argos is full.

Tonight's dinner was a small pizza I purchased at a nearby store and then microwaved in the communal kitchen. You aren't allowed to cook in this kitchen, but you can use the microwave to warm things up. Some of the other guests staying here paid for the Pilgrim's meal and are down there now eating a menu of lentils, ensalada and, of course, pan (bread). None of that appealed to me and I really didn't feel like being social this evening. Plus, dinner is never really served until quite late in Spain. I have noticed that businesses start to close down at around 2:00 or 2:30 in the afternoon for siesta and then they don't open up again until almost 5:00 pm and, most of the time, that is just for drinks and tapas. Restaurants don't start serving dinner until sometimes as late as 8:00 or 8:30 pm. I'm sorry, but by that time my body is rapidly shutting down.

Also, tomorrow is going to be a very long day; the longest I have walked on the Camino so far. I am doing pretty good with blisters but my big toe is causing me a bit of pain, so tonight I rest and tomorrow I will just have to take it slow – one step at a time.

When did I become so anti-social? That's a label I don't really like, especially when it comes to me. Untrusting, yes, but again, these attributes were never part of my original DNA. You only have to be burned so many times before you finally realize who you can and cannot trust with your thoughts and feelings, even for a slow learner like me.

I didn't have to read the medical report to know that some family members didn't believe me about the injuries I sustained in the accident. It was just a massive blow to know that they and our mutual doctor were sharing opinions about me during their appointments. And, isn't there an oath he took that prevents him from doing that anyway. He really was breaking doctor/patient confidentiality by discussing my issues with them.

They believe I have PTSD because they have witnessed the effects of my attacks but they don't believe I actually sustained any physical injuries. Even though there was proof documenting my physical injuries and, even though I was making alterations to my life because of my physical injuries, for some strange reason it was easier for them to believe I was lying than to believe I was telling the truth. Mental, yes. Physical, no.

I used to own a Harley Davidson and I loved riding it. There is just something about riding the back roads on a motorcycle that enhances all of your senses and gives you an added feeling of complete freedom. After the accident I tried riding my bike and when I got back home, my husband had to physically help me off of it because I couldn't lift my leg enough to do it myself. For the next four years I would continue to try, even if it was for only twenty minutes at a time and, as much as I still loved everything about riding this bike, it was becoming more and more evident that I just couldn't do it anymore. As heartbreaking as it was, I put it up for sale and, of course because it was in such amazing shape for its year, it sold within the week.

It was during a random visit (and before I read my medical records) where I was verbally attacked by some family members and a mutual friend. Not only was I called a liar, I was also called a fraud and told that I was the reason why vehicle insurance rates continue to go up. I was accused of defrauding our system and lying about my injuries in order to get a big pay out at the end of my court case. Everyone in that room, besides my husband, told me I was lying about not being able to work or ride my bike. They accused me of lying about everything I was saying I could no longer do because of the accident. To this day, I really don't know why I stayed there for as long as I did and, if it wasn't for my husband finally standing up to them and getting me out of that situation, I probably would have stayed even longer, subjecting myself to the verbal abuse just to convince them that I wasn't a liar. Isn't that strange?

I was later advised by my lawyer that during trial preparations, these family members had been called and refused to testify on my behalf because they didn't want to have to "lie for me."

There will never be anything I can say that will change their way of thinking and that's okay. Through all of this, I have learned that you will know who your real tribe is when things aren't all sunshine and roses. When life is good, everyone's good but, when the shit hits the fan, that's when people start showing their true colors. Even though it will forever be difficult for me to understand it, I have to learn to accept it. There have been times when I have wanted to ask, "Why?" but do I really want to hear the answer? Do I really need to know? The answer is always "No".

Having said all that, I have had to learn to be brutally honest with the people in my life. My husband can attest to that. I definitely pick my battles and have learned to let other things go. And not just things. I have also had to let go of people. Those I had previously called friends but who would eventually show their true colors. My new favorite saying is "Save the drama for your Mama". I'm too old for that shit. Some family members may have betrayed my trust, but they are still blood and I won't let them go. I want those family members in my life and I would do anything for them so I have learned to accept them, flaws and all.

So, when it comes to Garry, why am I having a hard time accepting him, flaws and all? The answer is because I need more from him than any other member of my family. Like my mom always tells me,

"In the end, it is just the two of you." Which, when you really think about it, is true. At the end of the day, it's just the two of us and I need to figure out if, at the end of the day, I want it to be just the two of us.

CHAPTER 10
May 29, 2019: Los Arcos to Logrono – 29 km.

Well, it was definitely a long day but it was a beautifully long day!

Toast and jam have become my favorite breakfast of choice and this morning was no different. It was really nice staying under the same roof as everyone else and seeing familiar faces as we all prepared for the day, which for me and a few others, started at 6:15 am. I walked alone for most of the morning and, as much as I tried to hold out and hold on, I finally broke down and peed on the Camino. When nature calls you need to listen.

Because my day starts early, I am unable to take advantage of all the suggested stops that my guidebook describes as "places of interest". These are usually churches, museums or various historical sites that just aren't open when I pass through. I try to make an effort to stop and admire their outside architecture, take a picture and reflect on their importance. There is just so much history and grandeur that sometimes I just get overwhelmed by it all. So, I find beauty in the little things. The various objects found on the Camino trail itself. All strategically placed by the Camino Gods, Mother Nature or pilgrims before me in places where only they would know is the ideal spot to put them. A few of them are:

The poppy fields. I had heard that the allure of the poppy fields and vineyards on the Camino were beyond compare, and I am sure they are, just not at this time of year. Some of the paths I walked on today were lined with the beautiful and brilliant red flower making it easy to imagine the sight they would make had the landscape been inundated with them. And, even when the path started to get a bit long, just noticing the difference these flowers made to the scenery was extremely uplifting.

The local gentleman sitting under a tree and strumming his guitar at a junction of the Camino where the flat surface I had previously been walking on met with a steep incline was the perfect invitation to stop for a rest, have some water, a snack and just enjoy the moment. Something I need to do more of. I keep telling myself that I am going to do this at my own pace but then I meet up with someone and we start talking and the next thing I know, I am either struggling to keep up with them or pulling back to stay with them. It doesn't help that I still have this fear that if I don't have people in my sights then I am going to somehow get lost.

The rainbow that appeared overhead which, in Western culture, represents a sign of hope and a promise of better times to come. The mound of stones handmade by others who had placed tributes in the form of pictures of loved ones they had obviously lost and who had probably been their source of inspiration for walking. Even the wooden sign I saw today that read "A Santiago 623 km," reminding me to be proud of the huge accomplishments I have already made and all the achievements I still have to look forward to. These, and so many more, represent the minute, yet huge entities that my eyes are now open enough to see, my mind clear enough to recognize and my heart willing enough to let in. Pretty deep stuff happening here.

The terrain itself continued to supply me with more uphill battles and downhill descents as I walked out of the Navarre region and into the Province of La Rioja. This is where the landscape changed and I found myself walking, with little shade, through several vineyards. Not surprising considering that La Rioja is well known for its local wine industry.

I had purchased an orange from one of the various vendors you come across on the Way and decided there was no better time to eat this orange than smack dab in the middle of a vineyard. I don't normally eat oranges at home, but my body has been craving the weirdest things and I wasn't about to deprive the body from getting what it wanted. So, there I was, walking alone in a field of bare wine making grape vines eating what I could only describe as the best orange I had ever tasted in my life. And when I say I was describing it, I was. I was actually describing it with words being spoken - out loud. Again, alone in a vineyard in the middle of Spain. That orange was, by far, the best part of walking through that vineyard and only because it is May and the vines were bare. The vines may not have been that impressive, but that orange sure was.

Arriving in La Rioja's Capital city of Logrono was impressive. The entrance to the city was over the San Juan de Ortega Bridge, a visually stunning bridge that was constructed in 1884. Not only is it a symbol for the city itself; it also appears on Logrono's coat of arms. Unfortunately, I had to walk an extra fifteen minutes off the Camino trail to get to my hotel - the Hotel Ciudad de Logrono. Beautiful hotel with a very modern room that even has a bidet, but, again, it would have been nice to be close to the hostels and albergues. There would be no running into fellow pilgrims here.

I did find a laundromat and was able to properly wash and dry all of my clothes. The other day I washed some of them in the sink and then hung them out the window to dry so it was nice to take them all and give them a good cleaning. Before leaving home, I purchased Pocket Laundry

Wash; thin and compact laundry sheets that are perfect for this type of adventure. Before this trip I had never heard of them, but so far, I have been impressed with their ability to keep my clothes clean.

On my way back from the laundromat I stopped at a supermercado and grabbed a salad for dinner. Recently, I have noticed a lot of people buying chocolate bars and now I know why. It's like I mentioned earlier, there is something about putting your body through this type of physical activity, day in and day out, that makes it crave things you normally wouldn't eat. I'm sure there is a more scientific definition for this but, again, I wasn't about to deny my body of its desires, so I bought a chocolate bar. One big enough that I can enjoy a few squares at the end of each day as a well-deserved treat.

I also got to talk to my mom tonight on Facebook and she passed on a few messages from Garry. 1. He spotted a deer in our yard back home, 2. He mowed the lawn until about 9:00 pm and 3. He loves me.

Through our conversation, my mom and I decided to set up a day and time I can video chat with him but, at this time, I really have no desire to turn on my phone and talk to anyone. I have messaged Kelly and video chatted with Lukas once, but I'm not even too sure if I have anything really to say to Garry. I have been putting daily pictures up on Facebook for the sole purpose of letting my mom know I am still alive and I also left her a copy of my Itinerary, which I know she is following along with back home, but I don't want to feel obligated to stay in touch with anyone.

I can feel that my emotions are all over the map and trying to explain, even to myself, the way I am feeling about anything right now is proving to be very difficult. This first week on the Camino has been physically exhausting and all encompassing. I have walked in the heat, in the rain, in the wind, in the wind and the rain, up steep hills and down steep hills and my body is constantly sore. I feel as if the Camino is purposefully tearing me down physically before moving on to me emotionally. Sure, I have shared a few things with people along the way, but it hasn't been to the extent where I feel I have made progress in coming to any conclusions or decisive decisions regarding any of my issues. At this stage, I feel somewhat accomplished if I am just able to complete a thought to its completion.

The only thing I know for sure is that I can't go back to the life I was living before I left and it didn't take me very long to figure that one out. I will take the blisters, the sore muscles and aching bones. I can handle the sleepless nights and the hill climbs that keep coming and I will walk barefoot if I have to in order to find some relief from a toe that won't stop throbbing. What I refuse to do is go back to the life I left behind. I am a week into this Camino and it is the best thing I have ever done for myself. I love it here.

To paint the picture more clearly, I want to give you a description of what I was dealing with before I took a break from my life.

Before the car accident and before meeting Garry, I was in a very physically and emotionally abusive relationship. For those of you who have been in one or find yourself still in one, I don't need to go into specific details for you to understand how toxic this kind of relationship is and yet how hard of a relationship it is to get out of. I had to literally run away from the home I had purchased and go live with my parents in order to escape that abusive relationship. I then met Garry and three years later we were married. While still trying to enjoy the honeymoon phase, I was in the accident that would greatly change the dynamics of our relationship. Five months after the accident, Garry and I purchased our first home. Although it is a beautiful property, it was, and still is, a fixer upper.

Approximately a year and a half after my accident, my brother started having his own health issues and, to make a very long story short, he was diagnosed with endocarditis, which meant there was a virus eating away at his heart. The medication he was given eventually shut down his kidneys and damaged his liver and the family was called down to the coast to say their goodbyes.

Put on dialysis long enough to get my brother coherent enough to hear his prognosis, he was discharged from hospital with a five-month expiration date. In six months, he was to be a first-time grandfather so he flat out refused to die and is still with us today. His story would take me on a yearlong journey of not only becoming his kidney donor but also an advocate to help save his life. I believe he is, or at least should be, writing his own book.

During this time, I had also re-connected with an old love who, during the course of our previous relationship, was diagnosed with a brain tumor. With the help of a few surgeries, he would go on to live another fifteen years but, when we re-connected, the prognosis wasn't so positive. I was with him at the beginning of his cancer journey and now I was facing the fact that I would also be there for the end. He passed away seven months before my trip to Europe.

Six months before my trip, my brother would go in for open heart surgery. We had finally found that one doctor who, in all good conscious, couldn't just sit there and watch my brother die without at least trying to save his life. He was a true miracle worker.

Four months before leaving, my husband had his heart attack. A case of heartburn that just wouldn't go away. Once again, I buried all my emotions and went on auto-pilot. Can't drive for a month, I'll drive you everywhere. Can't work, I'll work more. Need something, I will go get it. Have to do something, I'll do it for you.

Three months before leaving, I had the nervous breakdown.

CHAPTER 11
May 30, 2019: Logrono to Najera – 30 km.

     Today was a rough one. I got lost once but thankfully I was with Emily at the time who not only had an App that helped us get back on track, but she also speaks fluent Spanish and was able to talk to a local gentleman who was able to point us in the right direction.

     The Camino can be very hypnotic, especially when the scenery is monotonous and you find yourself entranced by the sound your feet and walking stick make as they hit the surface of the trail. It is very easy to just zone out. We had been walking along the side of the road when I turned around and noticed that the people, I clearly knew had been behind us, were no longer there. By the time we realized this, we were only about fifteen minutes off the actual route. We had literally walked right past the marker that was somewhat hidden in the long grass; leading everyone else to the left as we continued straight.

     What made the day especially difficult for me was that not only was it the farthest I have had to walk since I started, but it was hot and, like usual, I had worn way too many articles of clothing. Plus, walking on pavement is much harder on my body than walking on any other surface and today there was quite a bit of pavement.

     Having said that, today also brought more vineyards, parklands and beautiful scenery. The highlight was the lake I passed earlier on in the day that reminded me of home. Mornings are the perfect time for getting out on the lake and I have several wonderful memories of early morning fishing excursions with my family. The air is fresh and crisp, the sun is just starting to rise, the water is crystal clear and the haunting call of a loon is the icing on the cake. While walking past this lake, I felt as if

I were walking through a living and breathing piece of art and I made sure to take in every beautiful brush stroke.

With the continued fear of getting lost on the trail, I made an effort to follow a couple of women who were slightly ahead of me. I quickly noticed that they were totally oblivious to the gorgeous sights around them, and as I continued to slow my pace down to enjoy the views, I found myself getting farther and farther away from them. There were fishermen lining the rock wall between the lake and the walkway and I stopped to watch one of them reel in a fish. I saw squirrels and rabbits and took in the sounds of the birds. But the moment I will always remember is when my path crossed with one of a swan.

Now, these two women in front of me were damn near speed walking and as I watched them come to this small bridge, I noticed a swan swimming in the lake. He was a fair distance from the bridge itself and as the women approached it, he swam further away from them. It wasn't until I started getting closer to this little bridge that he turned around and started swimming towards it. It is hard to describe without having actually seen it yourself, but the closer I got to the bridge, the faster he swam towards it. I reached the edge of the bridge just as he was beginning to swim under it, so I stopped just before my feet touched its surface. This angelic bird swam under the bridge and right to the edge of the water where I was standing looking down at him. For just a brief moment in time, we were both just sharing space and, I truly believe, sharing a moment. He didn't even flinch when I took out my camera to snap a couple of pictures of this significant moment my Camino had just given me. It wasn't until I started making my way over the bridge that he continued on his way as well.

My experience with the swan was so meaningful to me that I would later look up its meaning. A swan's entrance into your life signals a time of altered states of awareness and the development of intuitive abilities. A time to accept the healing and change that is starting in your life. A reminder to go with the flow and listen to your inner knowledge and intuitions. The water it was gliding on was just an added bonus because water is linked with the feminine intuition and emotion.

I understand that some people's belief systems are different than others and I respect that. I have always been a curious person and enjoy listening to others as they describe their thoughts and beliefs, without judgement. Well, I always believed, or at least stated, that my spirit animal was the bear. For no other reason than I love bears. But I was so intrigued by my experience with this swan that I also looked up the meaning behind having a swan as your spirit animal. It is written that if a swan appears in your life, you should not ignore it. I didn't read that until after my experience with him, that's how powerful that brief encounter was. I couldn't ignore it.

The meanings behind having a swan as your spirit animal or totem:

- *You should slow down something in your life.*
- *Relax and let the Swan guide you, "go with the flow".*
- *Leave all the past behind you and start a new phase in your life. All the wounds from the past will be healed thanks to your spirit animal.*
- *Follow your intuition and believe in your own instincts.*
- *It is a symbol of transformation. You will have many changes.*
- *Of course, swans are a symbol of love, so your angels are sending you a message of love.*

These are just a few of the meanings behind the swan; however, it was very clear to me that this particular swan came to me when he did for a reason and this would be one of a few moments along my Camino that would have the most impact on my journey.

And to make this moment even more goose bumpy, while writing this (almost three years later), I went back to the pictures I took for reference reasons and when I clicked on the one I took of the swan, I was at first, reminded of exactly how close he allowed me to be to him but as I looked more closely at it, my eyes were drawn to something else. Where the water meets the shoreline, there is a particular stone half submerged under water. The part of the rock that is not submerged has the distinct outline of a heart.

Even though the vineyards haven't been as pretty as I had hoped, again due to the time of year, I am still finding beauty in everything. Whether I am walking through an industrial area or across railway lines, beside car dealerships, through wineries and gardens or even along the side of the road, I am exactly where I am supposed to be. I even walked past the ruins of the San Juan de Acre Hospital, founded around 1185 as a hostel and a place to aid pilgrims. As I rested my aching toe and enjoyed one of the best smoothies I have ever tasted in my life, I wondered what luxuries those pilgrims were afforded during their time of rest. Those thoughts were interrupted by a random neighbourhood cat looking for some cuddles. He reminded me of one of my own back home.

My room for the night is at the Hostel Ciudad de Najera, which was a little hard to find because it is tucked away on a quiet dead-end street that backs up against the red rocked cliffs that still house the actual caves people used to inhabit. One such cave can be seen from my bedroom window. If I had the energy, I could take a short trail leading up to these caves for a better view but, I don't have the energy and am happy with what I can see out my window.

After settling into my room, I met up with Cameron and we visited the Monastery of Santa Maria la Real. It was definitely worth the €4 we were charged to enter. Cameron's vast knowledge of the church made the experience that much more interesting and enjoyable. This monastery is supposed to be one of the most beautifully architected buildings along the Camino and it comes with crypts, caves and tombs. I'm sure those who have an eye for architecture would have been more impressed by the buildings design but, I'm not going to lie, I thought the crypts, caves and tombs were pretty cool.

I joined Cameron, David from Anaheim and Adam from Dublin for dinner this evening. A €12 Pilgrim's meal that consisted of a salad, pork chops and ice cream. Even though it was a lot better than the one I had in Roncesvalles, it still wasn't all that great.

David was a young man I had met on day six as I was walking out of a random town. I saw a young man in front of me walking extremely slow and I, like everyone else, walked right past him with just a quick glance and an even quicker smile. He was in his late twenties maybe, carrying only his camera and some water and walking as if every step was the most painful step he had ever taken.

After passing him I instantly felt guilty, like I should have turned around and, at the very least, shared in a few minutes of conversation before carrying on. But I didn't and I continued to feel bad. It was during the evening I stayed in Los Arcos and was having that beverage with Paul that I saw David limp into town a couple of hours after everyone else had. As he went to pass by, I kindly stopped him and told him how I had passed him earlier on in the day and how bad I had felt. I then apologized for not having slowed down and engaged with him for even just a short time. Apparently, he had fallen a few times on the trail from Roncesvalles to Zubiri and was really struggling with some injuries he had sustained but assured us that he was taking the advice of some nurses he had met. We invited him to join us, but he had had his bags transferred to the next town and was going to continue before it got dark.

I continue to have some shin splint pain in my left shin and, of course, that big toe is still throbbing away. I have just completed my stretches for the shin splints and now have my feet elevated with a cold cloth on my shins in lieu of an ice pack. I have also worked on a couple of blisters that are forming on both my baby toes. Thanks to all the research I did before leaving for Spain, I came equipped with all the necessary tools. Needle, thread, Polysporin and the proper type of band aid specifically designed for the toes. The goal is to keep the blister open enough so the water can't build up. The worst thing one can do is pop a blister because that just leads to infection so, you thread the needle and then poke it straight through the blister and then tie it off. A dab of Polysporin and a band aid and hopefully I will be good to go in the morning.

CHAPTER 12
May 31, 2019: Najera to Santo Domingo de la Calzada – 21 km

Today's walk only took me five hours to do. I left the hostel at 6:45 am and arrived in Santo Domingo de la Calzada at 11:45 am. I am not saying that to brag because I am not proud of this accomplishment at all. As much as I would have welcomed the breaks on this stretch, I didn't take very many of them at all. This was only because my feet were hurting so bad and I was afraid that if I took my shoes off, I wouldn't be able to put them back on again, or even want to put them back on.

It is suggested that when you are resting, you should take your shoes off and let your feet breathe. Even better would be to soak them in a nearby river. And if there isn't any natural cold water around, you should elevate them when taking a break. I knew they would feel better once they were out of the socks and shoes and into my sandals because usually when I do that at the end of the day, my feet become so much happier. I guess that's why I pushed it as hard as I did in the hopes that relief would be coming sooner rather than later.

I walked alone most of the day and I welcomed that solitude as an opportunity to privately and silently work through the pain and struggles I was going through for the better part of it. Not just the pain and struggle of my feet but also the inner struggle I was battling with the "shoulds." "I should be resting more," "I should take my shoes off," and "I should be taking better care of myself."

Today seemed to be just a continuous gradual climbing kind of day with very little to no shade and most of it was done while walking along a straight dirt track. At times, the trail was touched by a cluster of poppies to give the scenery a splash of color and even though a lot of it felt very monotonous, I was still able to find a bit of humour despite all the pain I was going through. When I wasn't concentrating on all the discomfort, I would play a game with myself where I would see a fellow pilgrim quite a distance ahead of me and wish I could trade places with them. Usually, one who had just conquered a hill. After climbing the same one, I would turn around and imagine that the pilgrim behind me in the distance was wishing they could trade places with me.

I did meet a lady from Holland who is walking the Camino with her dog, Flo. At times, Flo would keep pace with me and at others, she would just come by for a quick cuddle and then be on her way. Watching Flo do her thing reminded me of a thought I was beginning to adopt just before departing for Spain. One that I began saying quite often, "I think I am starting to like animals more than people." Was I just becoming jaded or were my eyes finally starting to see things more clearly? Most people have their own agendas and, very rarely, will someone do something for you just because. Animals are trusting, non-judgmental and provide unconditional love and companionship with no strings attached. They have no other reason for being by your side other than they just want to be. Today, Flo was there to pick my spirits up and put a smile on my face. She made me forget the pain I was in by distracting me with her antics and, in return, she asked for nothing.

I know that there are a lot of people who, like me, will go out of their way to help a loved one or even a stranger out for no other reason than to make that person's life just a little bit easier. Whose own life is more fulfilled when they are doing for others with no agenda or strings attached. This is just how I was made. I love coordinating family functions that take way too much time to organize and that set me back financially just so that I can sit back and watch the people I love play the silly games I have created and enjoy the food I have prepared. To hear them laugh and see them come together and enjoy each other's company as a family is priceless. I am the one who will purchase a coffee for the person behind me in the drive-thru just because, by doing so, it might make them smile. I am also the one who will be first in line for the tests that will show if I am a kidney match for my brother, no second thoughts or questions asked. It is just the right thing to do when you are built like me. But things were changing and I didn't like it.

When I wrote that the majority of people have their own agenda, won't help unless there is something in it for them or, in my case, were becoming less trustworthy and very judgmental, this observation or what was becoming my truth was, again, years in the making. What was sad though was the realization that they, meaning the people I had surrounded myself with, had always been that way. I was becoming so focused on the negative that I literally felt I was rotting from the inside out. It was as if I was screaming at the top of my lungs for help and, not only were they not listening, they were turning their backs on me. Me, the one they knew they could always count on. Me, the one they knew would always be there for them. Me, the one they knew would drop anything just to get to them in their time of need. What about me? You owe me!

So, this was what it felt like to have an agenda and, obviously, expectations.

February's nervous breakdown was chaotic, destructive and mentally and physically draining. It was also the beginning of my "Fuck you" attitude. The "I don't need anyone" mentality. The three remaining months after my breakdown was being lived in survival mode. I literally walked on that plane in Kelowna on May 20, 2019, emotionally and spiritually broken.

Arriving into the village of Santo Domingo de la Calzada early in the day allowed me the luxury of exploring its one thousand years of history. Cameron and I toured the Cathedral which was erected directly over the tomb of the hermit, Santo Domingo de la Calzada. Inside is the famous chicken coop that is home to a rooster and a chicken (which symbolizes a local legend) and, although I could hear them throughout the building, I never did see them. I later learned that I had been looking in all the wrong places. I was too busy looking "around" when I should have been looking "up". The ornate chicken coop is actually built into one of the walls.

The architecture of the Cathedral was incredible and I found myself particularly struck by the mosaic and tile designs throughout the building and, thanks to a tip from David, Cameron and I found the door that led us up a narrow spiral staircase and into even narrower passageways.

It's one thing to read about it in history books, but there is just something about actually walking through the tapered defensive walls of a seven hundred- and eighty-five-year-old medieval Roman Catholic Church that gives it a little bit more validity. We were literally walking around in the space between the building's outside and inside walls. The narrow passageways that Cameron and I found ourselves getting lost in were the same corridors where Roman Archers once took their posts to defend the church and the enormous amount of riches found within it. And although I am extremely fascinated and overwhelmed by this all, I can't help but be a little sad as well. The church had to be built with these false walls in order to accommodate battle "stations" to protect the people and the wealth inside the church itself, but what about the people outside? There is way too much wealth inside these buildings that very easily could have been shared with townsfolk. Greed is an ugly thing.

This evening, I am staying at the Hostel Rey Pedro, located right in the center of the city. I have a beautiful room facing the street with a mini-balcony that I used to hang my clothes to dry after washing them in the bathroom sink. But most importantly, I am using this time to take care of my shins and my feet. Today was a massive wake-up call that I am not doing enough when it comes to listening to my body. My two feet are what's going to get me across Northern Spain and if I don't start listening to them, they just aren't going to make it.

There is a farmacia and supermercado right across the street so, after purchasing some supplies, I came back to my room and went to work. I couldn't find any Epson Salt to soak my toe in so I purchased some coarse salt instead. I then lined one of the drawers from my night stand with the plastic bag I was given at the market, filled the drawer with hot water, added the salt and soaked my feet. I purchased a Compeed gel toe sock that I have stuffed my infected toe into with the hope it will provide some relief and have re-sewn the two blisters that don't seem to be healing. I also bought some Compeed toe separators to keep my toes from rubbing up against each other. That has now become an issue and probably the main reason those blisters won't go away. Hopefully this will make a difference. Last but not least, I have done my shin splint exercises which are becoming increasingly more difficult to do thanks to my big toe. I am currently laying on the bed with a pillow under my calves and cold towels on both of my shins.

I am ready for tomorrow.

PS: I have to include this now or I will probably forget in the morning. Before retiring for the night, I grabbed my clothes from the balcony and noticed that they probably weren't going to be dry for the morning so I have hung them in the armoire with the door closed and a blow-dryer on high inside with them. I believe I have made my own little version of a dryer and am hoping my clothes will be dry before I turn the light out for the night.

CHAPTER 13
June 1, 2019: Santo Domingo to Belorado – 23 km.

I have officially completed one-third of this Camino. As proud as I am of my accomplishments to date, it's also a bit scary because, at times, I don't feel like I have "truly" completed one-third of this Camino. This phase has been extremely physical which is congruent with all the pre-Camino research I read and despite all the suggestions posted about not going into this with any expectations, I am starting to feel like I did. I guess I am just feeling like I should have had more pronounced revelations about my spiritual and emotional journeys which seem to have been overshadowed by the more obvious physical toll my body has been going through. I am also feeling a little saddened that one-third of this is done because I really don't want it to be over.

My guidebook advised me that today would be a tranquil day filled with a series of small villages and it definitely was. Leaving the province of La Rioja and the vineyards behind, I walked into the Province of Burgos today and the high plateau of Castilla y Leon.

I decided last night that instead of leaving my hiking sandals in my main suitcase, I would carry them in my daypack so they would be readily available if needed them. I had read that after your days walk you should take your sneakers off and put on something more breathable as well as comfortable for your evening activities. In my case, it is becoming more obvious that I need my sandals during my walk as well. I find that my sandals provide my feet with more room to spread out, meaning my toes don't constantly rub against each other. I would rather have happy feet than be concerned whether or not I look silly wearing sandals with socks. Walking the Camino is far from a fashion show. Packing my sandals in my daypack was the best decision I made because I needed them. I lasted most of the day in my sneakers but the last 5 km were done in those sandals.

Today was a bit of a continuation of yesterday where most of it was spent on wide dirt tracks, wide open spaces consisting of rolling farm lands and, again, very little shade. The difference though was that there were more small villages to walk through and, unlike yesterday, I took those breaks I needed. During those breaks I also took my shoes off and elevated my feet. Even though it hurt getting my shoes off and hurt even more trying to put them back on, I know these are the things I need to do to make sure my feet are getting the care they desperately need.

Today was also spent enjoying the company of others. I walked with Kim and Emily and ended the day alongside Cameron, which was a nice treat because, even though I have been spending time with him after the walking stage is done, I hadn't shared any part of the Camino trail, itself, with him before today.

Prior to arriving in Spain, I made the decision to leave all my labels and titles behind and just be a girl named Colleen from Canada and I feel that's exactly who I was today. Today, I really felt like I embraced the whole vibe and meaning of the Camino. I took my time, I listened to people and opened up to newfound friends. And when I say that I listened, I truly listened. With the absence of any and all other distractions, I made sure to give the person walking beside me the respect of my attention as they spoke their truth. Today, I genuinely smiled and laughed. I spent time contemplating what the Camino was providing me and I soaked it all in.

One thing a pilgrim can count on during a long day on the trail is an inspirational message left behind by another before them. These words of wisdom can be found written on wooden posts in felt pen, spray painted on the walls of an underpass or even strategically placed on a random rock. I decided, at the end of this extremely physical portion of the Camino, that I would write my own little inspirational message on an object adorned with many other words of wisdom. My message simply read, "YOU GOT THIS :)." These three small words weren't just written for the people who will pass by them for years to come but a gentle reminder to myself that yes, I got this. I can do anything.

Arriving into Belorado was a real treat. I walked into the Plaza and was instantly greeted by a random juggler. It was like he deliberately met me at the entrance to the village with his own personal style of a "Welcome!" It turns out there is actually a festival being held here with music, rides, food vendors, performances and beverages.

My lodging is the Hotel Jacobeo located right on the Camino and is equipped with a bar and an outdoor seating area. During check in, I ran into a fellow Canadian who I had remembered seeing a few days ago but had not spoken to. He would be pretty hard to forget considering he is pretty much covered with beautiful tattoos. We introduced each other, exchanged some pleasantries and then went our separate ways. I was still in a social and, now, festive mood so I quickly unpacked and made my way back to the Plaza.

After enjoying the entertainment of the festival, I returned to the hotel and was pleasantly surprised to see Jack, my fellow Canadian, sitting outside having a drink. I asked if I could join him and we ended up visiting for longer than even I expected.

If I was a skeptic before, I am no longer one. I honestly believe my Camino is showing me everything I need to see and telling me everything I need to hear. Jack also suffers from PTSD – Post Traumatic Stress Disorder. His is much more debilitating than mine due to his extended period of time in the military as a combat medic. He is a retired hero who served our country for fifteen years; ten years shorter than what he would have wanted. A medical discharge proved him unable to continue his duty. Together, we shared our reasons for walking the Camino and talked about our various tattoos and the meaning behind them. We discussed our families, some of the crazy adventures we had been on and also shared our hopes that we would see each other in Santiago.

He did not talk about his fifteen years in the military other than to say he has seen and experienced things no one should ever have to see or experience. And when he described the effects his PTSD has had on his life and the symptoms he has, I felt validated.

Not only did this validate my struggles, it also normalized them. The "shame" of having a mental health issue began to fade away and I found some hope in his words. It was very obvious to me that his entire life has been affected because of this, but I was most struck by how positive he was. I am sure it took a lot for him to get to this point and I am even more sure there are some things that will never go away but he, admittedly, refuses to dwell in any sorrow or woe. I don't believe I have ever "sat in my sorrow". For me, it is more embarrassing. I'm afraid of having an attack in front of strangers because of the lack of understanding around this type of thing. Being stared at while being in such a vulnerable state. It also sucks that I have to make sure I always have my medication on hand and an escape route ready just in case.

I am just so glad I was given the opportunity to discuss this with someone who can totally understand and relate and, for that, I will forever be grateful to my fellow Canadian peregrino, Jack.

Some people may be triggered by what I write next, but nevertheless, this is how I felt before talking to Jack and I am sure there are others who, after reading this, may feel just as validated as I did that day.

Talking to someone who has experienced the same things you have has more validity than someone who has never been where you have been. Before talking to Jack, I felt like a freak with a mental disorder. I felt stupid and no longer in control of my common sense. There were certain incidences or triggers that would, and still do, cause an attack that I felt a "normal" person would just logically know could never happen and, because of that, I felt like I was losing my mind. To me, anything bad that could potentially happen was definitely going to happen. I hyper fixate on it and then become hypervigilant. For instance, just after the accident I would go for a twenty-minute walk every day and during that twenty-minute walk, all I would think about was all the bad things that, not only could happen, but were probably going to happen. Having convinced myself of all these terrible possibilities, I would then mentally and physically start preparing myself for the worst. A bear was going to come out of the woods and kill me, the car coming in my direction was going to swerve off the road and hit me, the dog barking behind the fence I passed was going to jump over it and attack me. Sometimes I would need to call someone to try and talk myself out of this fear, other times I would start to cry and sometimes I would just turn around and go back home.

I couldn't be in a crowded area, not only because of being extremely claustrophobic but because I was terrified of getting trapped. I had a paralyzing fear we were all going to have to start running for our lives and I would be trampled on or, even worse, I would be separated from the person I was with and I wouldn't know how to escape and then I would die. To this day, I avoid driving behind a semi-truck because I believe its trailer is going to come unhitched and slam into me or that whatever it is carrying is going to fall off the trailer and hit me. Those thoughts, although extreme, are normal and very plausible to me at the time and, no matter how much or how hard someone tries to explain my fears away, common sense no longer makes any sense whatsoever.

Again, those certain people in my life who don't believe my physical injuries, believe my mental health issues and I feel it is only due to the fact that most of them have seen one, or more, of my panic and anxiety attacks. Believing I have PTSD and anxiety is one thing and, as much as I appreciate the help and support I am shown during an attack, I feel that just "believing" may not be enough.

Mental health conversations are hard ones to start. It is one thing to watch someone, like myself, struggle through an "episode" but it is another thing altogether to understand the disorder itself. I can appreciate the sensitivity around approaching a mental health conversation and when I have been faced with it, whether about myself or someone I care about, I started the process by researching, reading and obtaining as much information I could about whatever the condition was. There is so much more behind the "attacks", just like there is more than just the outwardly or clear signs that someone has a mental health disorder. It's the part of the illness you can't see that should be talked about without shame, embarrassment or judgment. Believing is just believing but once there is knowledge there is understanding that then leads right into compassion, sympathy, tolerance, adjustments and change. Understanding has the power to create emotions that will hopefully lead to tearing down the "stigma" of mental illness.

After talking with Jack, I really felt the need to advocate. I am not too sure what that will look like for me in the future, I just know that this is something I feel very strongly about. For those who may be reading this and have been diagnosed with some form of mental health disorder, or haven't yet been diagnosed but feel that they may have some form of mental illness, please know that there is no shame in it, you are not alone and if you haven't already done so, seek help. Also know that this may be something that you HAVE but it is definitely not who you ARE. You are not your illness.

I am not embarrassed to say that after returning to my room this evening I soaked my infected toe in a bidet. It wasn't my first choice but there were no other options available to me in this room. I then doctored up some of my blisters, did my leg stretches and am now tucked away in bed with the hopes of a good night's sleep. If all my documentation is correct, tomorrow is going to bring me more hills to climb.

CHAPTER 14
June 2, 2019: Belorado to San Juan de Ortega – 24 km.

I began this particular day with a special Birthday recognition to my Uncle Bill. He would have been seventy-two years old had he not tragically died at the age of thirty-eight in a river raft accident back in 1985.

I had arranged for certain members of my family to take part in a river raft race that was being held in a neighbouring town. My brother, twenty-one, my sister and I, both seventeen, and my uncle took part in what I thought would be a fun family event. With the help of some rope, a couple of inner tubes and a small blow-up raft, we concocted an eclectic floating device and set sail first thing the following morning with my father, grandmother and my uncle's seven-year-old daughter as our cheering squad.

The start of the event proved to be entertaining as we all found our spots on the raft and worked towards synchronizing our movements for optimum performance, but it became pretty clear almost from the start that the river's rapids had more control of our "ship" then we did and, for the most part, were moving in the direction it wanted to take us in. Although we were able to maneuver our way past some of the potential hazardous barriers and obstacles we found ourselves faced with, we did not miss the log jam. The force of the rapids had turned our raft around and because of that, the back of the raft made impact first. My brother was able to scramble on to the top of the jam but unfortunately my uncle, along with my sister and I, were all thrown into the water. Landing on top of my uncle as I entered the water is something I will never forget. I was immediately thrown under the log jam and remained stuck underneath it for what seemed like hours. It wasn't until I stopped struggling and my body went limp that the rapids whisked me forward and I was able to swim to shore. In spite of the fact my sister was the first person I saw when I emerged from under the water, she too had been stuck under the log jam and, like myself, can re-live and re-tell that moment like it happened yesterday.

I can't tell you what happened to my uncle during his time underwater. I can say that the last time I saw him alive, he was clinging to our overturned raft and yelling for help. The current then carried him around a bend in the river and that would be the last time I would ever see his face or hear his voice again. The many incompetency's of the organization in charge of the event are too many to list. Let's just say a lot of things happened that day that never should have happened, including the death of my best friend. As the three of us stood on the bank of the river trying to make sense of what was happening, we watched as the "rescue" raft hit the same log jam and, again, throw its occupants into the river as well. Those men would all swim ashore and, as a group, we walked out of the forested area to the side of the road where police officers were waiting. It was on the side of the road, standing behind a police cruiser, that I was told my uncle didn't make it. While his kids were sitting in the back of a police car being driven to where he was, my father was retrieving his brother's body from a fishing boat and carrying it to an awaiting ambulance. We then had to drive home without him and then explain to a seven-year-old girl why her father was no longer with us. And, although our collective and individual lives before the accident were far from perfect, that day would prove that things could always get worse – and they got worse.

William James Holland was not only my uncle, he was my best friend and, on quite a few occasions, he was the only person who could keep me sane in an insane environment. Not only did I feel the tremendous void of his absence, I was also living with being the one who was to blame for his death. Of course I blamed myself; I was the one who organized the event. What validated my thought process at that time was the fact that some of my family members were blaming me as well. Others vehemently tried to take this burden off of me by explaining the whole thing was just an extremely unfortunate accident but a few of them held on to the blame. One, in particular, went to her grave believing it was all my fault. It took an extremely long time but, thanks to the help of some grief counselling both group and private, I was able to let go of that blame. It was a horribly unnecessary and unfortunate accident, that's all it was.

My day started at 3:00 am thanks to a big toe that won't stop throbbing. I hate to say it, but the pain is becoming more and more unbearable as the days go on. The agony of putting my shoe on is excruciating. Once my foot is in the shoe, I am given temporary relief but, God forbid, I kick a rock or stub my toe along the trail.

I decided this morning that this foot needs a lot more attention than I can give it and if I have to visit a clinic or hospital to get some antibiotics for this obvious infection, that is what I am going to do. The hard part is finding a clinic or hospital along this particular part of the Camino. The next "big city" is still two days away.

After doctoring up my blisters and cramming my red throbbing toe into my sneaker, I got away early enough that I was able to take my time and still arrive in San Juan de Ortega mid-day.

I just want to share the reason why I had waited so long before I made the decision to search for medical advice or treatment.

I had spoken to an acquaintance of mine prior to my departure who had walked this particular Camino a couple years prior. The purpose of this conversation was to obtain some tips and suggestions as well as to discuss some of my trepidations and anxieties towards the journey I was about to embark on. I had asked her about clinics and hospitals and she shared what she claimed to be her own personal experience on the matter.

She advised me that she had a blister that, over time, became so troublesome she had to seek medical attention. To make a long and, somewhat, unbelievable story short, she said she spent five days in hospital and eventually had to have a skin graft. In her words she "now has Mexican skin on her foot" which, not only to me, is an offensive thing to say but it is also incorrect. The correct term for their nationality is Spaniard and the main ethnic groups are Spanish, Moroccan and Romanian. Also, if you are in need of a skin graft, the surgeon will take it from your own body rather than the skin of a stranger. Although I asked to see them, I was never shown any pictures.

So, it was because of this tale and the fact I was now suffering from an obvious infection that I began asking those around me who I knew were also suffering from extremely harsh blisters what their thoughts were. To paint the picture even clearer, you don't have to look very far for people presenting with foot problems on the Camino because you see their feet and the destruction the Camino has had on them on a daily basis.

Not only were they forthright about their personal experiences but, if they didn't have their own, they shared someone else's and after listening to quite a few people, I came to the conclusion that what I was told back at home was probably not all that accurate. It's true people go to clinics for their ailments but, from what I gathered, the cure for severe and/or infected blisters is either buying two bottles of wine and taking a few days off or stop walking, go home and try again another time.

I am not saying the doctors don't take this seriously because they do, and I definitely believe people go to these clinics for treatment. What I am saying is that the conclusion I formed after talking to several people, researching the topic online and dealing with my own issues was that I wasn't going to a clinic or hospital until I had exhausted all other avenues. And I just want to add that there are several avenues to take, which led me to question how she let her alleged issue get so bad she actually needed a skin graft. There are pharmacies everywhere and, even if there isn't one in the particular village you overnight in, there are several you pass by during the day. And, let's say there wasn't, there is no doubt in my mind one of your fellow pilgrims was packing around a small medicine cabinet full of supplies that could have helped until you did find the next pharmacy because I was one of those pilgrims. I can't even count how many people I helped with the medical supplies I had with me.

By the way, those toe separators didn't work for me. Even when I taped the two toes together, the gel separator still found its way out from in between them. And I definitely couldn't walk with the individual gel toe sock on. That just made my toe throb even more.

Today's section had been described as having a bit of everything. A few steep inclines, some road noise and the last of the magnificent forested scenery as I start moving closer and closer to Northern Spain's Meseta.

I made sure I took several breaks including one in Villambistia, where I sat in the courtyard by a pretty fountain with four jets and an iron cross. It used to be the main water source for the villagers, but the water today is no longer drinkable. Leaning my walking stick next to me so that I could snack on a banana and take the occasional sip out of my now dented green water bottle, I took a minute there to ponder all the material items I possess back at home that I feel I need. Do I really need all that stuff? There, in Villambistia, all I felt I really needed was the banana, my green dented bottle filled with water, my walking stick and these shoes that are trying their best to keep my feet safe. You never know what thought or question will come to the forefront while taking a well-deserved break and, in that moment, that was the question.

Climbing this one section that can only be described as a thin and rocky foot path lined with tall grass and brush on either side, I could hear what, to me, sounded like someone listening to a Spanish opera song. As I got closer, it became evident that on the other side of a brick fence was a private residence. This only became more evident when I walked past an opened door leading into, what I could only assume, was the owners beautifully manicured back yard. The aesthetics were so breathtaking I actually took a few steps back so I could take a picture. Above the door read "Perro Suelto" which means "Loose Dog." I neither did see this dog or the gentleman who was either working in or enjoying his garden while actually singing this beautiful tune.

The part of the day I was looking forward to the most was a long section in the woods I had seen several times on YouTube and it did not disappoint. When I arrived at this particular stage, I found I was completely alone. I want to believe the universe and my guardian angel had joined forces to make this moment happen for me as there literally wasn't another soul around. Just me, the sounds of birds chirping in the distance and the ominous yet beautiful wooded area reminiscent of any Disney movie where children go off in the woods they were told not to go in. I took a moment to soak in my surroundings and enjoy the time given me before other pilgrims arrived and then I just carried on.

The trail soon became rather steep and once at the top, the forest opened up into a wide logging road. With make shift benches and inspirational messages fashioned by sticks, rocks and other materials found on the path, one could tell that these gestures were mere attempts at beautifying the littered remains of a deforestation site. I did like the "I LOVE <3 U" creatively made with sticks in the middle of the pathway. It was definitely picture worthy.

I had been walking for some time and my body was telling me it was time to take a break. The only problem was, at that specific moment, there were no make shift rest stops, no benches, picnic tables or even a large rock to be found on either side of this wide forest road to sit and have a rest. When I finally hit the preverbal wall, I literally just pulled over on the side of the trail, sat down on the dirt next to a tree, took my shoes off and enjoyed a snack and some water. I was tired, sore and needing this part of the Camino to be over and it showed. A gentleman passed me and, as he did, he looked down at me with total understanding. He looked just as tired. I shrugged at him as if to say, "You gotta do what you gotta do," and he smiled and nodded in agreement and that was the extent of our communication.

As I walked into San Juan de Ortega, the first thing I noticed was a small albergue with a bar/café attached to it. Outside were several occupied patio sets, so, before even attempting to find my accommodations, I asked to join a group of people I had met along the way. I had no idea how much farther into town I had to walk to reach where I was staying, all I knew was I was in desperate need of a Coke Zero.

I also learned today, through talking with people, that there might be a chance I can purchase antibiotics at a pharmacy without first having to go to a clinic, so I was anxious to find one. But it didn't take long in my conversation with the people I was now sitting with to realize this village is way too small to have anything resembling a pharmacy. With only three options for a room and two options for a meal, this village has very little else to offer. In fact, I had been staring at my hotel the whole time I was enjoying my Coke Zero because it was literally right beside the café I was sitting at.

I immediately gave up on finding anything that would ease my pain, at least for this evening. But then something amazing happened. One of the gentlemen sitting at our table told me that tomorrow would be his last day on the Camino. His journey was ending in Burgos. He said his daughter had given him some antibiotics "just in case" and, while shuffling through his bag, told me he wouldn't be needing them anymore. Once found, he handed them to me with the hope they will provide me with some relief. Another wonderful and weird example of how my Camino is looking out for me.

I am, by no means, trying to advocate the actions of accepting drugs from strangers. This was purely a personal decision I made under the circumstances. There are no strangers along the Camino, just friends you haven't met yet and, as a woman walking the Camino alone, I had been asked many times if I felt safe and the answer is always a solid "Yes!" You become an instant family the second your trail runners or hiking boots hit the surface and you automatically feel this sense of security, safety and community. So, when I was offered the antibiotics, I took them with no feeling of intended malice or harm but, rather, of generosity and kindness. I also want to make clear that when I got to my room and hooked up to the free WiFi, I did look them up online and researched the ones I had, paying close attention to the usage and effects.

My accommodation is at the Casa Rural Henera, which sits next to the village's Monastery. In order to check-in, I had to walk to a nearby bar/café owned by the hotel and, having announced my arrival, I was escorted back to the hotel by the manager. The property itself is surrounded by black aluminum fencing that gives off an air of sophistication while at the same time, announces its total separation from the albergue beside it. Meaning, if you aren't staying here or don't have the intention of staying here – don't even bother.

The WiFi connection is very poor, with the only hotspots being either in the common room or the courtyard. Each night I have been giving my mom a virtual tour of my room but today, she had to be content with a showing of the garden and my laundry, which was hanging on the line to dry after being washed in my room's bidet. I feel no shame in where I wash my clothes just as long as they look and smell clean when they are done.

I end today's writing in total awe of my surroundings. Never once in my wildest dreams did I ever imagine myself sitting on a deck somewhere in Northern Spain soaking up what is left of the sun's warmth all while watching my clothes dry on a clothes line. The breeze has picked up a bit making the clothes sway back and forth in a somewhat hypnotic motion creating even more of a "Norman Rockwell" or "Hallmark" vibe.

The first batch of antibiotics have been taken with the hope my toe will soon be on the mend. My whole body aches, my shins or sore and my blisters, though not getting any worse, aren't getting any better either and yet, I can honestly write that I am the happiest I have been in a very long time.

CHAPTER 15
June 3, 2019: San Juan de Ortega to Burgos– 28 km

This morning I did something I haven't done this whole trip. I actually left the hotel without having seen any other person pass by first. It was just after 6:00 am and still somewhat dark, but I felt like going so I did. As I very slowly and quietly closed the gate behind me, I looked up and saw a fellow pilgrim step out onto her balcony, still in her night clothes and with a beverage in hand. Before walking away, I waved at her and she waved back. But it was more than just a wave, it was a "Buen Camino" and a "See you on the Way." It was an all-knowing gesture of her wishing me well just as I was wishing her. A hope for a day filled with the insight to see and embrace all that our respective Caminos were going to provide us.

The physical stage of the Camino is now just becoming a daily acceptance. I very well know that when I sit down to take a break, some part of my body is going to hurt when I finally make that slow attempt to stand up. I'm acceptant of the routine of doctoring up blisters, padding areas for more comfort, remembering to stretch before beginning the days walk and soaking my toe in anything I can find once the day is done. And, as much as I am accepting the physical part of this, I now know, especially after today's walk, I am starting to break through and embrace the emotional stuff as well.

This morning was absolutely magical. The path out of the village led me to an oak forest where I felt, for at least the first forty-five minutes of my walk, like I had Spain all to myself. Besides the occasional cow who would literally cross my path, it was just me and the sounds of nature. It was heaven. The air was crisp and the mist was cool but the chirping of the birds and the movement of dark turning to light was breathtaking. The spell I was under broke long enough for me to realize I hadn't seen a Camino marker in quite some time and, even though the thought of being lost entered my mind, I wasn't panicked by it. I was fine with just "going with the flow" and seeing where this path was taking me. What finally broke me from the trance I was in was the faint chime of a bell that only meant one thing, I was no longer alone.

I don't even know what this man's name is but he has become very well-known thanks to the bell he has tied to his backpack. I believe he is from Italy and doesn't speak a word of English but I found out, through someone else, that this gentleman has done this particular Camino at least seven times. Whenever his wife goes to visit her family for long periods of time, he packs up and walks the Camino Frances. He wears the bell so the people in front of him will be warned of his impending arrival, allowing them ample opportunity to get out of his way as there is no doubt, he is walking this Camino faster than anyone I have seen so far.

As I walked towards the town of Atapuerca, I was greeted by a sign stating this was the home of Europe's oldest human remains believed to be some eight hundred thousand years old. This piece of information just blows my mind. I walked through the town way too early in the day to make any kind of inquiries about visiting this historic site but apparently it is a cave where over sixteen thousand fossils, including nearly complete skulls, have been found. Just knowing I passed one of the most important archeological sites in the world is hard to grasp but also knowing I may be walking on the same path that people did over eight hundred thousand years ago is hard to soak in. I am just feeling so extremely blessed and somewhat honoured.

At some point after Atapuerca, I was faced with a very steep and rugged uphill climb, a struggle I shared with another Italian fellow. He was forced to abandon his valiant attempt at conquering this feat on his bike and dismounted, pushing it the rest of the way up this steep mountain of jagged, uneven rocks. I can't even say this section of the Camino even resembled a clear path at this point. It looked more like the aftermath of a mudslide without the mud. A mudslide of jagged and uneven rocks. It then turned into a bicycle tire sized trail leading through the trees and I started questioning if I was still going in the right direction. At least I had the Italian man in front of me to follow. And I know he was Italian because when I was younger my dad taught me a lot of Italian curse words and, today, I heard most of them come out of this man's mouth as he fought to push himself and his bike up and over this very difficult section.

Even though I found this part of the Camino challenging, it was hard to dwell on the pain it was causing my feet or the energy it was taking to continue the climb purely because of how beautiful it all was. The placement and color of the stones reminded me of places I had visited in Arizona and the fact that the trail abruptly transitioned itself from a clear path to a rock wall you had to climb followed by a thin line zig-zagging itself through a small wooded area was really quite exciting.

At the top was a make shift cross where pilgrims had placed stones, trinkets and photographs under. I had come prepared to leave something at the Cruz de Ferro and, having seen the Cruz de Ferro online, I knew this wasn't it. But I had brought something else with me as well and immediately knew this was the perfect place to leave it.

Traditionally, pilgrims carry a stone from home that symbolizes their sins or burdens. Having carried the weight of those burdens throughout the Camino, they then leave the stone and what it represents behind at the Cruz de Ferro. I decided to take a piece of coral my grandkids had picked out for me during a trip they had recently taken to Hawaii. I wanted to leave something positive at the Cruz de Ferro instead of something negative and, again, a personal choice I had made ahead of time.

I also brought along a crystal that had been given to me by someone I thought was a very close friend. I chose to bring this crystal because I believed it held the lies and deceit that came with the person who gave it to me. It was by chance I actually found it while preparing for this trip. The instant I took it out of its satchel, I knew it had to come with me. And not only come with me, it had to be left here with the intent of throwing it away, along with everything it represented. It was dark, heavy and gave off such a negative energy. I believe that crystals choose the person not the other way around and I never really felt attached to it anyway, so the decision was an easy one to make. Into my daypack it went and it would stay there until I felt the time was right to let it go and today was that day.

Standing at the cross and perusing over some of the other items left behind, I was approached by my rock-climbing partner and asked if I would take a picture of him alongside his bike with the wooden cross as his backdrop. A forever reminder to commemorate his victory to the top. After he left, I found the crystal and placed it amongst the other items with no particular thought or strategy as to where its final resting place would be. I knew why it had to stay as much as I understood why I had to carry it for as far as I did. Then, without any fanfare, I snapped one picture and started getting ready to move on.

What happened next was another sign that these stages don't happen in the sequence we read about when researching the Camino. It had been a very physical day thus far. Even though I can feel my body is growing accustom to the intense work out I now do on a daily basis, today had been a real hard one and it wasn't even over. I still had the downhill portion to do. But when I put my daypack back on, I could physically feel it had become noticeably lighter. Or, was it that my soul had become lighter? It was definitely a spiritual moment that could not be ignored. In that moment, I felt a sense of enlightenment and freedom. I stood in that moment, allowing it to resonate and then I took a cleansing breath and carried on.

This illuminating moment was soon followed by another. I was faced with a very steep and rocky downhill grade and, of course, during these sections of the Camino it is very important to pay close attention to every step and foot placement to prevent the risk of falling and injuring yourself. I was just beginning my descent on a very unsteady and rough piece of terrain, putting all trust in my walking stick to provide me the stability and support I desperately needed when out of nowhere, all my trepidation was replaced with a strong sense of protection. I instantly felt so connected to this stick and confident in its ability to lead me safely down this hill. I knew, no matter where it was placed, it was going to guide and support me the whole way down. It truly felt as if my dad, Frank, was holding out his hand and helping me down one step at a time.

I don't believe I've yet to cry on the Camino but today I cried like a baby. There was only one other person around when the tears started flowing but I didn't care. There could have been a whole crowd and I still wouldn't have been able to keep it in. I cried and cried and then I cried some more. I even turned my phone on, which I knew I would be charged for, just so I could call home and tell my mom what I had just experienced. My infected and blistered up toes were burning, throbbing and screaming at me but I felt amazing!

Up to this point, I hadn't really obtained many answers to a lot of the questions I had coming into this but what happened on that mountain is something that will stay with me for as long as I live and the feeling that came over me is something I will never forget. I actually got an answer to a question I didn't even realize I was asking and it didn't take me long to decide what I was going to do about it. As I continued walking down the mountain using a stick Frank had bought specifically for me and specifically for this reason, a stick that now had become a symbol of the love, support and guidance he has always shown me, I decided I wanted him to be my dad and not just my step-dad through marriage, but my dad. I told myself that when I got home, I was going to look into Adult Adoption.

It took some time to research all of my options and, after talking with a friend of mine who happens to be a lawyer, it turns out it is a lot more difficult to do than I had hoped. I thought I could just have a lawyer draw up the necessary documents and then present them to Frank in a creative and surprising way and then, if he accepted, all he would have to do is sign them, file them and that would be that. I was wrong. First off, the "child" in the matter can't start the application process, the intended parent has to. Then, we would both need our own legal representation, our respective spouses would need to file their own documents and the cost involved would be extremely high. Instead, what I decided to do was have a Moral Adoption Ceremony. I made up some legal looking documents and a Certificate of Adoption and presented them to Frank on Father's Day – a year after returning from Spain. I had invited him over to the house along with my mom and grandmother. We were all sitting outside under a tree having some snacks and enjoying each other's company when I gave him the gift. He was totally speechless once he realized what it actually was and there wasn't a dry eye there. Of course, he said "Yes" and now we both have our nicely framed Certificate of Adoption hanging in our homes. But most importantly, the man who, through his own actions, dedication and continued selfless acts of love bears the title he deserves. In my heart, my mind and my soul he is my dad. There is no other.

I had read that the approach into Burgos would be a tough one and it was. Walking on pavement, at the best of times, is much harder on the body than walking on the trail and this was definitely not the best of times for me. My feet were telling me they had had enough. The area I was in reminded me of walking through certain parts of downtown Vancouver with the busy sidewalks and even busier traffic and I found that the whole experience was bringing up some anxiety. You don't realize how much you appreciate the silence until you are abruptly thrown into the noise. So, when I noticed that some other pilgrims had stopped at a café equipped with picnic tables, I joined them. While taking my sneakers off and replacing them with my sandals, I overheard some of the conversation they were having and, putting two and two together, I realized they were actually waiting for the city bus. We were sitting near the bus stop and they were waiting to be driven the rest of the way into Burgos' city centre. Because of the anxiety this stretch of the Way was giving me and the continued pain I was having, I made the decision to join them rather than walking the remaining 6 km to "Old Town" Burgos. I definitely made up those 6 km in my attempt to locate my hotel, which was beautifully tucked away within the historic centre of the city. I also did quite a bit of sightseeing.

Entering Burgos through the Arco de Santa Maria is an experience all of its own. The Arco de Santa Maria represents one of twelve magnificent gates that once guarded the walled city of Burgos during the Middle Ages. Walking through this beautiful stone carved entranceway makes you feel like you are walking through time itself. It doesn't take long to realize this is a city that begs to be explored and that's exactly what I did for several hours after my arrival.

I visited the very impressive Cathedral. Dedicated to the Virgin Mary, construction of this masterpiece started in 1221 and wasn't completed until 1567. It is also the resting place of El Cid who was a legendary Castilian Knight. His tomb sits alongside his wife's. The Cathedral's two towers can be seen from just about anywhere in Old Town. I strolled along the River Arlanzon that separates the old part of town from the new, I sat in the Plaza Mayor and people watched and, whenever I felt I was lost, I just looked up to find the two huge towers of the Cathedral and headed in their direction.

My lodging tonight is at the Hotel Rimbombin, a very modern and beautiful hotel situated in an equally beautiful location. My step counter is showing I have taken close to forty thousand steps today which is also evident in the intensity of the pain I am feeling in my big toe. After soaking it in a garbage can and tending to the issues I am having with my two pinky toes, I have made the decision to give my feet a well-deserved break tomorrow and take a taxi to Hontanas.

Even with some of the issues I am having, I believe my pre-Camino foot care is definitely paying off. I have seen people with blisters all over their feet. Blisters on the top of their feet, on the bottom of their feet, on the side of their ankles and in between each individual toe. Blisters that have become infected and, sometimes, even blisters on top of blisters. My two main issues are, of course, my infected big toe that has now turned three shades of purple and the blisters that I have on both pinky toes, so I think I am doing pretty good. I have tried separators, tape, needle and thread, bandages and a combination of all of those things but nothing seems to be working. I am 100% certain had I purchased sneakers a size larger than I normally wear, I wouldn't be in this predicament. But, the truth of the matter is, I am in this predicament and I need to do what is best for my feet.

Tomorrow's walk is essentially the starting point of the Meseta – Spain's high plateau desert. It is also written that this is where a person's emotional journey is supposed to begin. It consists of long stretches with little change in scenery, little to no shade or shelter and where just being alone with yourself and your thoughts are bound to drive you a bit crazy. Many people, including a father and daughter team I met on the train from Paris to Bayonne, choose to skip this section all together. I don't want to do that. I want to walk as much of this path as possible so I have to be smart about this and do what I feel is right.

Tomorrow's stretch would also have been the longest I would have walked to date. It is a 31 km day and I have been told that the climb up is hard but the trek down is a lot harder which is making the decision to take a cab an even easier one. And, unlike the first time I had to make the tough choice not to walk a particular section, today's decision wasn't so difficult to make.

I wrote a lot in my journal about the expectations I obviously came in to this with and most of the time those expectations centered around all the questions I had about my life, my choices and where I felt I was going or where I should be. I guess I assumed that if I plunked myself as far away from all my distractions and entered a world of silence and serenity I would easily and quickly find all the answers. I remember another story this person with the "skin graft" had shared with me prior to my departure. She said it was during the Meseta or "emotional" stage of the Camino where she found she was able to mentally grab hold of one of the issues that brought her to Spain, focus all her energy on just that one issue, work it out to its conclusion and then move on to the next.

I can't really say I had the same experience. I had a tremendous number of random issues, words, thoughts, opinions, beliefs and doubts rolling around in my brain, especially during my time on the Meseta. I came into this on the wave of a nervous breakdown, so I was still trying to focus on forming sentences in my mind let alone solving all my problems.

But it was while I was working my way into Burgos where I made the decision not to walk the next day and that was when I was reminded of her particular story. I may not have been able to pick out a specific issue and deal with it until I had come up with a solution but I was experiencing moments of clarity that would just come out of nowhere and instantly feel right. Depending on a walking stick to help me down a mountain BOOM – I want Frank to be my legit dad. My feet are killing me today BOOM – don't walk tomorrow. And this particular day had been an extremely emotionally and physically draining day. The day prior, my foot was hurting so bad I actually had to take my shoes off and, for about 2 km, literally walk on the side of the road in just my socks before finding a safe place to sit down and change into my sandals. Not something I would recommend but, at that moment, it felt so damn good. I also remember that when I made the decision not to walk the 31 km to Hontanas, there was no inner battle with the "shoulds." It actually felt just as good as taking those sneakers off and walking in my socks. Maybe, after twelve days on the Camino, I was starting to shed the excess baggage I had brought along with me.

CHAPTER 16
June 4, 2019: Burgos to Hontanas – 31 km

I will start with a continuation of last night. After completing what is fast becoming my nightly routine, it ended with me laying on a very comfortable bed with two pillows propped under my calves to elevate my feet, cold cloths on both my shins and, at various times, an infected toe soaking in a waste basket all while watching the movie *Rocky* in Spanish and no subtitles. Most of the time I don't even turn on the TV, but I knew I didn't have to wake up early this morning so I turned on some mindless television and stayed up a bit later than usual. No pressure or guilt, just pure relaxation. It was amazing.

Following a leisurely morning in my room, I went back out into the city in search of a "real" cup of coffee. During my exploration last night, I had walked past a Burger King and was really excited about heading back there this morning for a cup of Joe, but to my disappointment, it didn't open until noon and I was standing at their doorway two hours early.

In the effort of allowing my feet and each individual toe the chance to breathe and stretch out, I traded the constraints of trail runners and socks for the comfort and space of my sandals. What a difference small changes can make. I casually walked around Burgos expanding my walk to areas I hadn't seen yesterday and then found a small café situated in a quiet corner of the square and ordered a café con MUY leche and it really wasn't all that bad. It didn't take very long before I was joined by Emily, Scott and the rest of their crew.

I had a really enjoyable conversation with a young lady by the name of Rachel whose plan is to join a convent in California after completing the Camino. Like many, she is searching for answers and guidance from God while still being open to new experiences and living in the moment. Her goal is to reconnect youth and young adults to religion and, I believe, with her determination and personality, she will succeed in her chosen path.

While returning to my hotel, I bumped into a gentleman I had spoken to along the Way and, after comparing injuries, he suggested I purchase a pair of hiking toe socks. He was actually on his way to a sporting goods store to buy something for his hamstring injury and invited me to join him, so I did. I am open to trying anything that may help the cause so, with a new pair of lightweight toe socks in hand, I arrived back at my hotel, packed up my belongs and by noon, I was in a cab heading to Hontanas.

I can't speak to how the trail was today, only to say that my guidebook expressed that it would be a challenging walk with a series of ups and downs and a lot of distance to cover. Reading that was one of the deciding factors in my decision not to attempt it. The cab ride was longer than expected and it was made even longer by the fact my driver didn't speak a word of English and I don't speak much Spanish. He did try his best to occasionally point out the route the Camino trail was taking and, just as I was beginning to think he had taken several wrong turns in an attempt to jack up the fare, we had arrived. And, he actually charged me less than what the meter read.

Hontanas lies in a hollow and is totally invisible until you are practically right on top of it. Because of its compact size, it didn't take long for me to locate my lodging for the night which is at the Hostel Funetestrella. Like so many of the other hostels that provide private rooms, I had to first register at the main building that has the lobby, all the shared accommodations and communal breakfast/restaurant area. I was then escorted to a separate building where all the private rooms were located. Situated on the main street along the Camino route, the window in my room afforded me the luxury of watching my fellow pilgrims make their way into the village in search of a bed.

After exploring the village, which took all of ten minutes, I was directed to a path that led up to the highest point where I was told, offered an enjoyable view of the area. I grabbed a Coke Zero, an orange and my journal and made my way up there. The view was beautiful and, true to form, provided me with a bird's eye view of the entire village. I took a seat on one of the three plastic lawn chairs and began journaling. When the wind picked up a bit, I set aside my journal and just enjoyed the peace, solitude and the view.

During my brief walkabout, I noticed that each albergue (there were three) had their own Pilgrim's menu and, after reading over each one, I decided I would dine at my own albergue. Dinner would be at 7:00 pm followed by an evening of live music. As sure as I was of this impending plan, I did not sign up for a seat at the table because then I would be committed and obligated. Two things I just didn't want to be. Continuing my walkabout, which really just consisted of walking up and down the same road, I noticed David, Adam and a few other familiar faces were sitting outside their albergue enjoying a beer, so I joined them. This would turn out to be the highlight of my day.

The main street is so narrow you can have a conversation with the person sitting on the opposite side of it without having to raise your voice. On one side of the road were three small round plastic tables and chairs and, if you had three people to a table you were really pushing its limitations. The opposite side of the road provided more shade so people had lined their plastic chairs up against the adjoining buildings. The entertaining banter bouncing back and forth was hysterical. There were jokes being told, beer being drank and laughter being had. The Italian gentleman who wears the bell on his backpack began imitating everyone's style of walk, including mine and, although I couldn't understand a word he was saying, his actions were all I needed to see to enjoy a laugh alongside everyone else. Every once in a while, David would try to interpret what this gentleman was saying, but it really wasn't necessary. This man was so animated he didn't need anyone's help at all to get his point across.

As I sat there enjoying the company of strangers the more at home I felt. It's quite the phenomenon that happens the moment you step foot on the Camino. It just doesn't matter where you are from, what you do for a living, what color your skin is or what your sexual orientation may be. We are all equal. I totally get the fact that people change when they are away from their everyday stressors and responsibilities, but I want to believe how we are treating each other on the Camino is the true version of ourselves and that this version has just gotten buried or lost underneath all of those stressors and responsibilities. Maybe, what we are all really just looking for is balance. I know I am.

As the rest of the day wore on, the crowd that had gathered started to dissipate and, as much as I enjoyed the company, I still yearn for solitude and quiet, so I opted out of the dinner I, thankfully, didn't commit to and I retreated back to my room.

Taking the time off from walking and spending the entire day in my sandals has made quite a difference. I feel no guilt at all about my decision to skip this part of the trail and am really looking forward to trying out my new toe socks tomorrow. I have performed my evening routine of soaking my toe, tending to the blisters and getting everything ready for tomorrow. This includes packing my daypack, rethinking what I packed in my daypack, unpacking my daypack and then repacking it again. You would think I'd have this down pat by now but I don't, so instead of dwelling on it any longer, I will turn in for the night.

I hope I am not giving off the impression that I was ever lonely because I definitely wasn't. I wanted to be alone. I left home because I needed to be alone. As much as I want to say that I was searching for the person I had lost or had simply ignored for so long, I now feel that maybe what I was really doing was introducing myself to the new version of myself in whatever form it was going to take. And if I first made the choice to join people for a Pilgrim's meal and then later decided I just wanted to be alone instead, that was what I was going to do. I was going to honor how I felt at the time and just roll with it.

CHAPTER 17
June 5, 2019: Hontanas to Boadilla Del Camino – 28 km

Once again, my Camino has provided and I just have to continue to trust it. Had I chosen to walk yesterday I never would have run into that gentleman heading to the sporting goods store and I wouldn't have purchased those toe socks that have turned out to be a total game changer. What a difference it makes when each individual toe has their own separate living quarters. Those socks are exactly what the doctor ordered and I am just sad I didn't purchase a second pair.

It was because I was feeling so much better that I didn't take as many breaks as I know I really need to be taking. The weather played a factor as well due to the fact it rained for most of the day, but I honestly didn't mind all that much. My toes were happy and the scenery was amazing.

The visual eye candy began pretty much right from the start of my walk thanks to the Monastery of San Anton Ruins, a 12th century monastery once dedicated to caring for sick pilgrims as they made their way to Santiago de Compostela. Its enormous archway welcomed me into the abandoned village of San Anton that was first founded in 1146.

The pavement I was walking on soon came to an end and was replaced with a broad, earth track. Not only had this path been rained on for quite some time, but it had also been trampled on by the many pilgrims who had walked or rode their bikes and horses on it before my arrival, leaving me to fight my way through a muddy and very slippery mess. I actually chose to walk in a farmer's field that paralleled the sloppy mess setting a precedent for those people behind me.

I travelled past hilltop castles, admired the Romanesque churches that seem to appear in every small village or town I walked through and I strolled over the most spectacular medieval bridges. And, as much as I try to hold on to the mental pictures I am taking of these spectacular sights, they are all constant reminders of the sheer amount of history I am viewing on a daily basis. When thinking about it, it becomes somewhat impossible to believe I am actually here, I am actually seeing all of this and I am actually doing what I am doing. I become instantly overwhelmed at the magnitude of my existence right now.

The day started revealing the eminent change in scenery as I transition from the first stage of the Camino into the second. I play witness to the forested mountain region being replaced with wide-open spaces and wheat fields for as far as the eye can see and I am excited for the change. It actually reminds me of one of our prairie provinces back home and I know, for a fact, I won't have a problem looking at this type of view for the duration of my time in the Meseta. I find it calming, peaceful and quite beautiful in its own right. I have been so spoiled with my daily surroundings this entire journey and, as much as I love being in the forest or walking alongside a river, stream or lake, I know I will find just as much to be grateful for during this phase as well.

But, before the land turns completely flat, I was presented with yet another intense climb. Just like the Pyrenees at the beginning of my journey, from a distance this particular ascent didn't look all that challenging. However; the closer I got to it the more I was beginning to dread having to climb it. I remembered reading in my guidebook that there would be a small climb but what it forgot to mention was the fact I would be gaining over 100 metres in height in a little more than 1 km.

When I finally reached the top of this very steep climb, I stopped to catch my breath, take a picture of the beautiful views and celebrate my huge accomplishment. I was in the middle of a pretty good motivational and complimentary speak to myself that was, of course, being done out loud when I realized there was a woman sitting on a bench in a makeshift shelter not fifteen feet from where I was standing. We both just shared a laugh and I continued on.

Arriving in Boadillo Del Camino, I made my way to the Albergue en el Camino. I had read that this was a simple albergue with a lovely garden area and a small pool, and it was. But upon my arrival, I was escorted out of that beautiful little setting and brought to a separate building because, once again, the shared albergue is one building and the private rooms are in a separate one beside it.

Edwardo, the owner, advised me that I was getting the nicest and biggest room in the building and I truly think it was. It was a very nice and spacious room. I even splurged and paid the €7 to have my laundry done and, after washing my clothes in sinks, showers and bidets, it really is a treat to have them washed in an actual washing machine with real laundry soap.

After cleaning up, I walked back over to the "simple albergue" and enjoyed the rest of the afternoon and early evening with some of my Camino companions. Edwardo, his family and all of his staff do an amazing job of making a person feel right at home. The garden area was extremely inviting and it even included an outside eating area, which I found myself sitting in for the next four hours enjoying a Coke Zero, a piece of cake and the company of new friends.

What began as a table of four (David, Adam, Mike and myself) soon became a table of two and I found myself not only being opened up to, but opening up to a young man close to half my age. It's amazing what this journey does to a bunch of strangers with two commonalities – the walk itself and the search for something. David and I shared some time in, what I can only describe as, a mini-counselling session and I hope he valued it as much as I did. As I looked around and watched familiar faces make their way into the village and, specifically, into this particular albergue, it was becoming more and more apparent we were all silently becoming more connected with one another as people, as a group and as a family and maybe that is why we all feel so comfortable opening up the way we have been. I'm sure when David sat down at the table he didn't, for one second, think he would be sharing some of his extremely personal experiences with me just as it was totally blowing my mind that I was sharing some of my stories with him.

As much as I enjoy socializing with my fellow peregrinos, at the end of the day, it is nice to go back to my own room. A space I don't have to share with anyone else. A quiet and private place where I am able to process the events of the day without the interruption and noise that fill the walls of a shared hostel or albergue room. I am grateful for that.

My mom has always said that "advice" is better received when it comes from a stranger rather than a close relative and she is probably right in that assumption. In the past, I have tried to share my thoughts and feelings with various family members only to have them use those thoughts or feelings against me at their convenience. I'm sure I will get some kind of push back on that statement but, it is what it is. Or, if I ever did something "out of character" for me, those close relatives would judge me on my actions and then turn around and do something just as questionable or worse. And believe me, I don't think my family is any different than most other families out there. There is disfunction in all families. I just include these little facts of my life to show that you are not alone and that your family isn't the only fucked up one out there. And, like I had mentioned before, I feel there is more validation in the words of someone who has experienced or is experiencing the same thing you may be, so if you can relate to me, I hope I can provide you with that validation. You are not alone.

Back to this wonderful afternoon spent on a garden patio in Boadillo Del Camino. It just felt safer and more freeing talking to someone from another part of the planet, sharing things I hadn't shared with any other person and knowing this was as far as it was ever going to go. And even if they went back home and mentioned it to one of their friends, where is it really going to go? I will continue to believe that what was said on the Camino stayed right there on the Camino.

CHAPTER 18
June 6, 2019: Boadilla Del Camino to Carrion de los Condes – 26 km

Today was an emotional roller coaster ride. It began at 2:00 am when my mind decided it was going to start working overtime and it didn't stop for a break once. It must be the combination of all the sensitive topics that were brought up yesterday afternoon and the fact I am now walking through the emotional part of this journey. And, with little to no real change in scenery, it doesn't take long to jump right into your head.

The first few kilometers were, by far, the most beautiful. I walked parallel to the Canal de Castilla; a man made 200 km system that was built to transport the grain from the plateau region to the ports of Cantabria. There was still a mysterious morning mist in the air, the canal was lined with gorgeous elm and willow trees and the sound of the flowing water was mesmerizing. There were two gentlemen walking ahead of me and one following slightly behind and, as confident as I was about the direction I was heading in, I would still say I was kind of relying on the two men in front of me. Because of this, my guard was slightly down. It didn't take long for my blissful morning walk to turn into a bone of contention for the man behind me.

Like I mentioned before, the day started extremely early for me and I hadn't been able to shake all the worries, issues, family matters, questions and problems that had been rolling around in my head since 2:00 am. They were all still tumbling around in there fighting for the attention they needed. Meanwhile, I was trying to soak up as much of my surroundings as possible because it was really very picture perfect.

Somewhere in all of this inner struggle and outer beauty, I started to question whether or not I was still walking in the right direction.

I had paid enough attention to know the two men in front of me had continued straight at a point where you could either continue straight or take a pedestrian walkway across the canal and over to the other side. Having made the same decision to go straight, I looked behind me and saw that the man who had been following me had stopped at the crossing and was seeking the guidance of his map. It was because I was no longer one hundred percent certain I was now heading in the right direction that I continued to check behind me to see what decision this guy was going to make and, the last I had seen, he had decided to continue straight as well. It wasn't until I crossed a random road and back onto the path that I really started to doubt myself. The two men who had just minutes ago been right in front of me were now nowhere to be seen and the guy who had been behind me must have turned around because he was now on the other side of the canal and heading in the total opposite direction I was going in.

Feeling committed to the choice I made, I continued straight and, by doing so, I soon found myself staring at a dead end. The path literally stopped at a cement wall of an overpass. Even now, I have absolutely no idea where those two men who had been in front of me went. The choices were pretty limited – turn around and go back, which they didn't do, climb the cement wall, which was impossible, turn left into the bushes or turn right and swim to the other side of the canal. I made the obvious choice and turned back around. But the closer I got to the pedestrian walkway crossing the canal, the madder I got at the man who had been behind me. He obviously realized he was going in the wrong direction so, in turn, would also know that I was going in the wrong direction as well. Why didn't he call out to me, whistle or try anything to get my attention? He corrected his mistake before getting too far off the path so why not share that tasty bit of information with your fellow pilgrim?

I walked into the town of Fromista still feeling a bit irritated but was soon greeted by a stray cat who looked like he was in as much need of comforting as I was. I just love the sound of a purring cat and he did not disappoint. After providing each other with some cuddles, I attempted to walk away but he wasn't quite done with me and, if he wasn't walking right alongside me, he was in front of me crisscrossing my path and making it very difficult to continue without tripping over him. So, I would stop, give him some more love and then try my escape again. We did this little song and dance for so long I was starting to think I'd be stuck with this little fellow for the rest of the Camino but, eventually, he went his way and I went mine.

Feeling a little bit better after some cat therapy, I stopped at a small café for some orange juice and a well needed bathroom break. The stall was occupied so I stood patiently outside the door. From behind the counter, the owner of the establishment approaches me and, in Spanish, asked me if I wanted a coffee. I usually save my café con leche for when I am done for the day so I kindly said "No, thank you." What happened next was so random and so instant I really couldn't keep up with the fact it was really happening. He starts yelling at me, again in Spanish, and while he is doing that, his co-worker comes from behind the counter, stands right beside him and starts yelling at me as well. The woman who had been in the restroom opens the door and attempts to pass me the key but the man pushed me out of the way and grabs the key from both of our hands. And, while I am being pushed out of the way, the waitress is now barricading the bathroom door. Apparently, what he and the waitress were, aggressively, trying to tell me was that the restrooms were for patrons only and if I wasn't ordering a coffee then I wasn't using the toilet. I tried telling him that "Yo no bebo café" or "I don't drink coffee" and, instead, I would have a "jugo de naranja" or "orange juice," but it didn't matter what I said, he was not giving me the key. I actually had to pay for the orange juice I didn't even have yet before he would give me the key to the restroom. This whole scene was being played out in a very small and crowded café, which raised my anxiety and all I really wanted to do at that point was run out of there in tears. But, I didn't. I went to the restroom, grabbed my orange juice and my change, went outside, sat at an empty table and tried to process what the hell had just happened.

All day I would jump in and out of my head because there really was nothing around to distract me from my thoughts. The terrain was straight and flat with massive fields of corn on either side of this wide earth track leading me to Carrion de los Condes. And, even though the scenery never changed, it was still beautiful. Especially when the wind blew across the fields, sending the crops into a ripple effect like an ocean wave during a storm. And if the great coffee fiasco hadn't occurred, I probably would have enjoyed it more but, again, I was too stuck in my head to appreciate anything around me.

To gain some control over the jumbled thoughts circling around in my mind, I tried to focus on just one and give it my full attention, but it didn't work. My brain was in overdrive and there was nothing I could do about it. No matter how hard I tried, I just couldn't concentrate, so I decided to pop in my earbuds and try to drown everything out with a little music.

So, now I'm walking along this really long and straight track listening to my music and trying desperately to calm my mind, when I see an older Spanish gentleman carrying a walking stick and heading in my direction. Thankfully, there was a young guy ahead of me acting as a buffer between me and this older gentleman who was, very clearly, walking with a purpose because the moment their paths crossed the older man turned abruptly around and started walking alongside this, now confused, kid. I could tell right away this guy had no idea what the older man was trying to say. The Spanish man seemed to be talking a mile a minute and, every once in a while, he would raise his walking stick to point in one direction and then in the other. The young guy would stop to take a random picture and, when he did, the older man just stopped and waited. No matter what this guy did, he just couldn't shake this person. Then he did something brilliant. He took out his phone and, I believe, pretended to call someone because the second he did that the old man set his sights on me and now it was my turn.

I was about 4 km out of Carrion when he joined me and I think his intentions were to get me to stay at an albergue he was affiliated with but, like the young guy before me, it didn't matter how many times I said "no entiendo," Spanish for "I don't understand," he just kept talking and swinging his stick. It didn't matter how fast or how slow I walked he kept the same pace all while pointing his stick in one direction and then the other. I'm sure he was pointing at something in particular but I have no idea what it was. The whole experience was becoming frustrating and annoying and, just like the episode at the café, it was bringing up some anxiety. I felt like bursting out into a full-on sprint but was pretty certain he would have been able to keep up the pace. After several attempts at telling him I already had a place to stay, I took out my phone and showed him the name of the hotel I was staying at and, at that point, he turned around and went after the people behind me. What made the matter worse was, in order not to seem rude I had taken my earbuds out of my ears, rolled them back up and stuffed them in my fanny pack. At least that's what I thought I did. I have since looked everywhere and I can't seem to find them, which makes me think that instead of tucking them into the pack, I was actually tucking them behind it and they fell on the ground. This day was just one bad ju-ju after another.

I was so upset and frustrated that day and, I guess, the man at the café was just the final nail in the coffin. I don't know about you, but when people do things like that to me, I instantly feel a sense of guilt, even though I know I didn't do anything wrong. I had full intentions of being a paying customer at that establishment but it was like he was calling me a liar. This false sense of guilt is a personality trait of mine I wish I could get a handle on but, for some reason, it is deeply imbedded and in no hurry to leave.

And, I remember how hard I tried that day to narrow down one issue or concern of mine so that I could internally deal with it and let it go, but I just couldn't do it. It wasn't like I had to concentrate on the Camino trail because it was literally going in a straight line with enough markers on it that if you did get lost, you deserved to, so I did have the luxury of just zoning out and dealing with what was coming up. I guess my body just didn't want to deal with anything and I had to be okay with that. Just being okay with things that aren't working for me is very difficult for me to do and here is why.

In most family dynamics, each member has a role to play and my role was "The Fixer". When my alcoholic father (biological one) would slap my mom around, I would step in between them and save the day. I was around ten years old at that time and totally believed I actually could save the day. At least until the next time it would happen. It would continue to happen for six more years until my mom finally left. If there was a problem in the family, I had to fix it.

When my parents divorced and my sister left with my mom, I stayed with my dad. Why? Firstly, I stayed because I was searching for a Father/Daughter relationship I wanted to believe was there but it really never was and secondly, because I didn't want him to be sad. My job was to make everyone happy.

After my uncle passed away, we fought and won custody of his daughter. For the years I lived in this dysfunctional family unit, I played a major role in raising her. When I was finally strong enough to leave that environment, my father actually told this little human to rush downstairs in tears and beg me not to leave. I had to endure that for the length of time it took me to pack my bags and walk out the door.

I eventually got married and had Kelly and when I left Kelly's Dad and moved into my own place, I allowed her to move in with me. By this time, she was a teenager and very unhappy with her current living situation so, of course, I opened up my door to her. We made it work the best we could, a young single mother of a one-and-a-half-year-old baby and an even younger, and somewhat troubled, teenage girl. When it no longer worked for her, she left. I continued to allow her to walk in and out of my door and my life whenever and wherever, because that is just what I do. That's just what family is supposed to do, right? Again, I am the one who is supposed to be able to fix everything. And, if I can't do it the first time, then I just keep trying until it is either fixed or I burn out. I didn't "fix" her. I hope I helped her in some way but I know now there really was nothing more I could do other than leave my door open to her. And, she didn't turn out half bad.

As adults, my sister and I talked about how different our living situations had been after our parents split up and I was shocked to hear that she actually envied me This envy was based solely on the fact that my father bought me things. She had no idea. The only reason he bought me anything was to piss her off for leaving. It definitely wasn't out of love or guilt for saddling me with a seven-year-old child and an elderly grandmother to take care of while he was either away at work or at home too drunk to care. After my mom left and my uncle died, it became a living hell.

The ironic thing was I envied her as well. I envied all the wonderful stories she would tell me of the many cool things she would do with Mom and Frank. She was receiving the love and attention I was craving. I was actually forbidden to go over to my mom's house and I wasn't allowed to hang out with my sister, so I had to lie about where I was going, what I was doing and who I was doing it with. My place was in that hell house looking after my cousin, driving my grandmother around or drinking with my dad while he cried over the loss of his brother or bitched about my mom and sister. There was nothing to be envious about.

The man with the bathroom key may have been the last nail in the coffin but the other guy who wouldn't stop bothering me was the icing on the cake AND the cherry on top. I understood I had to trust the journey I was on and I knew the Camino was providing, but what on earth was it trying to provide me with that day?

All I was seeing, or getting out of it, was how much of a pushover I am and how I will ignore my own needs in order to appease someone else's. Why do I allow people to manipulate me and then treat me like shit? Why do I constantly say "Yes" to those who find it so easy to always say "No" to me? Why do I allow others to bully me, lie about me, lie to me and use me? Why do I allow them to talk shit about me behind my back, talk shit about me in front of my face and then bend over backwards to make their lives easier? Why am I waking up at 2:00 am worrying about all of this crap when they are all at home sleeping like babies? Do I become more like them? Do I just start taking and not give anything back in return? Do I start caring less? Do I start using people to get what I want and then discard them when I am done? Do I become a liar and a manipulator? Do I become heartless? Do I start saying "No" out of spite or start asking "What's in it for me?"

This was the kind of day I was having that day and those were the thoughts bouncing around inside my brain. That's the power of the Meseta. What I found frustrating was that I couldn't come up with the answers to any of those questions. It was frustrating because I am the one who is supposed to have all the answers. Again, I'm the one who is supposed to be able to fix everything.

Those few moments spent with those two men brought up SO much that day. I have worked through and have overcome a lot of traumas in my life – straight from childhood on. Then I was in the accident and I had a new trauma I was having problems working through. Like those two men, I felt like no one was paying attention to me, seeing my struggles, asking what my needs were. Like those two men, everyone just continued with their own agendas. Internally, I was screaming at the top of my lungs but externally I couldn't even get their attention long enough for them to even notice I needed help. I guess I was looking for things I had wished were there but, in fact, had never *really been there at all. It's like that Albert Einstein quote: The definition of insanity is doing the same thing over and over and expecting different results. Over and over again, I would hope for my loved ones to react one way and then be disappointed, angry and sad when I got the reaction, I knew, they would normally give. Why do I continually set myself up for disappointment?*

I can literally still feel the frustration I felt that day, it was a pretty tough one. And I remember trying to find my lodging for the night and getting lost several times within Carrion de los Condes itself. My offline map kept leading me out of town, across a bridge and into this very small residential area and, thinking I had gone too far, I would turn around, cross back over the bridge and continue searching. It turned out I had been going in the right direction all along and had literally passed by the place several times in this small residential area. Tired, dejected and feeling like this day had been nothing more than a total write off, I walked into my overnight accommodation and my Camino provided me with something amazing.

I can't even tell you what time I walked into Carrion de los Condes but it felt like I had been walking for two days. I was emotionally and mentally drained by the time I found my lodging for the night at the Casa Tia Paula and was seriously just wanting to put this horrible day behind me. Find something to eat, crawl into bed and forget this day ever happened. Walking into Casa Tia Paula was like winning the lottery and receiving a big ole comforting hug all at the same time. I could not believe my eyes. This place is literally a studio apartment equipped with a full kitchen, laundry, a living room with a small gas fireplace, king size bed and to top it off – a two-person jacuzzi tub! It also has a DVD player. The only drawback is that the one DVD I could find is in Spanish.

The first thing I did after picking my jaw up off the floor is put a load of laundry in and then I went out in search of some food I could actually cook in my very own oven. After returning with a chicken cordon bleu, I had a very long soak in the jacuzzi and finished up my laundry, which now smells so fresh and clean. I just finished taking care of my blisters and am now relaxing in bed. This place is exactly what I needed and, even though I didn't solve all my problems and even though the rest of the day was pretty shitty, there is no other place I would rather be right now then right here. I can't wait to see what tomorrow brings me.

CHAPTER 19
June 7, 2019: Carrion de los Condes to Terradillos de los Templarios –
26 km

Oh, the difference an Ativan and a good night's sleep can make. Again, I don't want to condone the use of drugs, I just find that Ativan helps calm my nerves and helps me sleep a little bit better. Something that is extremely important for my body and my mind. Most nights I don't sleep very well at all, waking up two or three times throughout, so I really notice the difference when I do get a good night's rest.

Even though I am noticing a difference in my stamina and my ability to handle more of the physical challenges of this Camino, my body has also learned to just accept certain things and keep on going. It's hard to explain it to someone who hasn't done a Camino or any other extended period of extreme and repetitive physical activity and, believe me, no one could have explained it to me either before now. I am just really starting to appreciate and admire what my body can do.

I honestly believe I will never be able to sit down for even just one minute on this Camino without needing two minutes to stand back up. My feet deserve medals for their tolerance of being jammed into these sneakers. A "feat" I sometimes forget until I replace those sneakers with sandals and feel what can only be described as, a little slice of heaven. I don't believe my walking stick will ever know the full extent of my appreciation for its strength and ability to hold me up when all I want to do is fall down and the daily shin splint stretches, as painful as they are, have now become mandatory in order for my legs to accomplish what they need to do during the course of a day. If I miss doing them, my lower limbs will still carry me to where I need to go, they just protest the entire way. And let's not forget the mind and the heart. The two driving forces that steer this ship. The strength it must take those two to drown out all of the pain and suffering and still have the power to convince the rest of the vessel to keep moving. Cheers to you both. I describe it jokingly but it is a fact. It is truly amazing what the human body can adapt to and accomplish.

I have to pause and explain a few things about my injuries. After posting daily pictures and descriptive paragraphs on Facebook for my family back home, my mom made a statement that I was making the Camino look too easy. Of course, she was joking because I was privately keeping her updated on all the difficulties I was having. And it wasn't like I had many, I mean, I feel very blessed in that regard. The physical difficulties I experienced are things I am sure many pilgrims either have or will experience during their own Camino.

The jet lag was a tough one. At a time when rest was extremely important, I wasn't getting any. While trying to catch up with that, I started getting body aches and cramps. I would wake up at all hours of the night with my legs already moving because they hurt so much. And when I talk about how wonderful it felt to just sit down, take my shoes off and put my feet up, it was. It was when I had to put those shoes back on, stand back up and start moving again that the suffering crept back in. There were many days where that was the toughest thing I had to do. And, not just physically. Finding the strength mentally can be just as painful.

The reason for the pause in this story though, is due to the part in my journal where I wrote how important the shin splint exercises were. After re-reading that, I was instantly reminded of what I actually had to go through to prevent shin splints or get a grip on the shin splints I already had. I started experiencing signs of shin splints pretty early on so I googled exercises that would help prevent them and I found as long as I did these five specific exercises at least once a day, I was able to keep the symptoms to a minimum. I had also started experiencing signs of that pesky infected toe on the second day of my Camino. That was, by far, my worst injury. An injury that caused me enough pain to keep me up at night, stop me from walking two stages of the Camino and one that not only stayed with me the entire trip but also long after I got home.

Now, getting back to being in awe of what the body and mind can do. If you look up the exercises recommended for preventing shin splints, you will find that all of them include poses where your toes are bent. In one, you are standing on your tippy toes and in another, you are actually sitting on your feet with your toes bent back. There wasn't one of those five exercises I could do without causing severe pain to my big toe, but I did them. If I wanted to continue walking, I sucked it up and I did them. I tried modifying them as much as I could, but I did them and I did them every morning and every night.

Again, I feel I got off pretty easy when it comes to the amount of Camino injuries I had because I did see people who were visibly struggling more than I was. And, even though I talk about "the body" like it is some entity outside of myself, I know that I put "my body" through a lot and the amount of drive and determination I actually had to walk across Northern Spain is very commendable. I don't want to take away how proud I am of myself for doing what I did but it really is amazing how united the body, spirit and mind become when there is a common goal and how they individually continued to push the limits and *boundaries of their comfort zones is really quite remarkable. A little pat on the back for me.*

Last night I read forward in my guidebook so I was prepared for the 17 km barren stretch that lay before me first thing this morning. With no villages between Carrion and Calzadilla de la Cueza, I made sure I was equipped with enough water and snacks to last the three hours it took for me to walk that particular section. Even though there were no villages, there was a small make-shift cantina called Bar Oasis out in the middle of nowhere that offered beverages and snacks.

The land walked on today was flat and offered very little to no shade. Besides the occasional Poplar or Oak tree, there were very few visual stimuli to keep a person from totally zoning out or getting into their head. What I found interesting though was that those three hours it took me to get to the first village seemed to fly by. I can't even tell you what I thought about during that time other than being very aware of the wind. The sun was out most of the day and, with no trees to block the wind, I felt every slap in the face gust of it.

What's misleading about walking on such a flat landscape is that, I could see the tower of the cemetery of Calzadilla off in the distance but it still took me an hour to reach the town itself. A small village with approximately sixty residents, Calzadilla de la Cueza offers little more than an albergue and a restaurant. Sitting at one of the restaurant's patio tables hugging the Camino path itself, I was able to watch as my fellow pilgrims arrived. As enjoyable as this section was, it was still a long haul and those of us who were already taking a well-deserved rest started cheering on those we could see coming in who looked as though they could use a little bit of encouragement.

It is pretty humbling to know that the rocky footpath that led me to this chair, the same path my feet trudged upon, was actually built by the Romans over two thousand years ago. It was their main road from Astorga, Spain to Bordeaux, France. To know my story now rests in the same stones that have absorbed two thousand years' worth of history is absolutely mind blowing. And, some may have issues with defacing objects or graffiti, but I continue to find inspiration in those messages left behind for someone, like myself, to read. Today's message was found on a stone along that long stretch of road this morning. The stone, itself had the shape of a shoe print and on it read, "But that is the reason I am here so no need to rush." Whatever the reason is, and there are several reasons why people are here, there really is no need to rush. So, I continued to sit in that chair and cheer people on.

With my toes once again tucked away in my sneakers, my green water bottle stashed away in the side pocket of my daypack and a firm grip on my walking stick, I carried on. I soon passed the ruins of what was once a pilgrim's hospital and, a little further on, a landmark representing the halfway point of my journey. At both, I stopped and reflected on where I currently was, where I have been and where I still need to go. Both stops ignited and stirred up some emotions which I am sure have now become their main purpose, especially during this phase of the Way.

This afternoon, I was joined by a Spanish gentleman who didn't speak any English. What was weird about our time walking together was that it didn't feel weird. It wasn't one of those moments where you walk side by side for a few strides as one person makes their attempt at passing the other, it was a deliberate choice on both our parts to remain walking together despite our inability to verbally communicate. The fact it didn't feel forced or uncomfortable made the whole experience so organic and beautiful. And, as I approached my albergue, I wished him a "Buen Camino," he said the same and then carried on his way.

My lodging for the night is at the Albergue Los Templarios, a new albergue located right on the Camino trail and about 1 km away from the village of Terradillos de Templarios itself. It has a very large grassy area which is ideal for sitting and hanging your clothes to dry on the lines available to the guests. Unfortunately, the wind was so bad the staff had to stack up the patio tables and chairs and put them away. My room is very nice and clean and their dining area is very spacious. Nothing to complain about here.

After cleaning up, I grabbed my book, my journal and a café con leche and, because there really isn't anything else to do here, I went outside to enjoy the sun while it was still shining. Because of the wind, I strategically sat in an area protected from the breeze and continued to reflect on the day thus far. It boggles my mind that one day I find myself stuck in my head feeling like nothing can go right and then the very next day goes as wonderfully as today went. Yesterday I felt like I had the weight of the world on my shoulders and, today, there was absolutely nothing pressing on my mind. I guess it's going to be a day-by-day thing and I just need to let it be whatever it is going to be.

I was joined by a few other people, including Jack my tatted up fellow Canadian, who were also seeking shelter from the wind but were just not ready to be inside. I gave up my chair to someone who hadn't brought one and found a spot on the grass to sit. The conversations were short and the silences were long but maybe it was because they were all still processing their day as I had been prior to their arrival. Or maybe we were just tired.

Once the sun went down, we all gradually made our way back in. I ate dinner alone in the dining room tonight, which was fine with me and have since retired to my room. I am noticing that all the people I am used to seeing, the ones who come along and break up my day with idle chit chat, are no longer around and that most of my time is spent in silence. It's not a complaint but rather a curious observation.

CHAPTER 20
June 8, 2019: Terradillos de los Templarios to El Burgo Ranero – 31 km

Today was another day filled with history, little hamlets and constant reminders that I am travelling the same roads others walked along in the year 955.

The transparency of the Meseta continues to let me dive into my thoughts as the terrain itself remains, for the most part, pretty level and predictable. For hours I find myself walking almost a straight line on a thin pathway paralleling the highway which, at times, becomes pretty monotonous. Like I mentioned last night, it hasn't gone unnoticed that for the last few days I haven't run into any of the people I started this adventure with. Besides Jack, who spends his evenings somewhat secluded, I have lost sight of any other familiar faces. I guess I got used to the routine of arriving at my final stop for the day, going out to explore all the things it had to offer and then stopping to chat with people I know - maybe even make plans to share a meal or tour a church or another local attraction together. Maybe my Camino is trying to tell me that now is the time for solitude, reflection and thought.

I did, however, share the first part of this morning with two sisters from Texas who are walking the Camino for religious reasons. The topics of conversation no longer surprise me on this path we are walking on because, like I have said before, it doesn't matter where you are from, the color of your skin, your sexual orientation or your religious beliefs – we are all here to get some kind of answer, some form of clarity, to rid ourselves of a burden, to feel an emotion we have been suppressing – we are all here for a reason. One of the ways to figure out that reason is to talk it out. These sisters were both under the age of twenty-seven and for the three hours we walked together, they shared their stories of sexual abuse and depression. Two topics I can definitely relate to and could easily have interjected my own thoughts, feelings and stories about, but I didn't. Instead, I listened. I did let them know that I am also a survivor of sexual assault and have also suffered with depression and that was only to let them know that I was a safe person to talk to and I could provide them with a knowing and understanding ear to listen with.

After 13 km together we parted ways in Sahagun, one of the few cities actually mentioned in the very first pilgrim's guidebook written a very long time ago. My travelling companions were going to wait until the Church of San Francisco opened so they could receive their halfway Certificate. I really wasn't interested in receiving that keepsake, plus, I was travelling farther then they were today so I stopped long enough to enjoy an orange juice and take in the welcoming sights of civilization that briefly replaced the vast farmlands making up most of these plains.

I walked the remaining 18 km alone and most of them were spent thinking about this morning's conversation. It truly doesn't matter how young or old you are, depression, anxiety and other forms of mental health issues can affect anyone. It doesn't matter how insignificant other people may feel they are; the issues that cause a person to become depressed or the reason why they suffer from anxiety; those reasons, triggers and causes are significant to the person being affected. They are very real.

I thought about all the really shitty and traumatic things I have experienced in my life. Sexual, mental and physical abuse, alcoholism, depression, anxiety, PTSD, divorces, accidents, deaths, my own near-death experiences – the list goes on and on. What I find interesting though, is that I don't consider any one of those things as the reason I am standing here today on an ancient path in Northern Spain.

I have touched on the issues I feel have brought me here but I can't say I have given them the time, thought and energy they deserve yet. Let's break them down. How much time have I spent thinking about my relationship with Garry? Not much. I can say right now that I am not really missing him and, besides our weekly video chats, I don't feel the need to turn my phone on and talk to him.

My grandmother is a woman I love very much, but I have to admit, she is another source of my stress. Every winter my parents, like the birds, head south for the winter. For the five months they are away, I feel it is my responsibility to watch over my grandmother. Yes, there are other family members who live just as close to her as I do but for reasons all their own, they have chosen not to make themselves available. Like many single elderly people, my grandmother has learned to distort situations in order to obtain the attention she needs and this causes me great stress. I know it is sad to say but I have to speak the truth. If my Diploma in Counselling doesn't qualify me to know what is really happening then it is the twenty-two years since my grandfather's passing that does. While he was alive, there was no real need for our support and, understandably so; they had each other to rely on. But, twenty-two years ago he left her alone, possibly lonely and in need of outside support. Again, totally understandable. I have spent a lot of time with this demographic and it is true that some learn to manipulate certain situations to get the attention, sympathy and support they miss when their significant other is no longer with them and most of the time, that form of attention is given to them when they are "sick" or "injured."

My grandparents weren't in my life much growing up. Even so, I felt very close to my grandfather when they were. There was just something about him that I was drawn to. He represented everything a man "should" be. Tall, strong and handsome. He was a man's man and he gave the best hugs. As far as having us kids around, his philosophy was we were to be seen and not heard and he made that very clear every time we were in his presence.

Although my grandfather survived a massive heart attack, his health issues eventually worsened and my grandmother became his full-time caregiver. He had always been her whole life so, this new role came naturally to her and if she had any complaints, she never spoke them, at least not to me. Needless to say, for the many years she concentrated her time and effort looking after him only meant that his needs overshadowed any of her own.

Just before leaving for this Camino, I was starting to become put off by her. I hate even writing this down but it is my truth and one of the reasons for bringing this journal. I just felt I was being manipulated by her. It was really taking everything I had to pick up the phone and talk to her and after hanging up, I always felt anxious and stressed. With those members of our family who reside a fair distance from her, she will engage in telephone conversations that are light and upbeat, never really burdening them with issues, problems or complaints. But then I will get a call from her where she sounds so horrible, I can barely understand what she is saying or she has gotten herself in such a state that I feel I need to rush over and fix things. I will become either extremely concerned or extremely exhausted by the whole conversation, feel guilty if I don't go over right away or will drop everything I am doing to tend to her needs. I am starting to feel less like her granddaughter and more like her caregiver. She has two children of her own, so this really shouldn't be my responsibility.

As much as I feel I haven't touched on this particular issue, the more I move through the different phases of this journey and the more I listen and talk to others; sharing our experiences, stressors and thoughts, I am beginning to feel a bit different. I have heard other stories similar to mine when it comes to elderly family members and, if change is going to be made in this relationship, it is going to have to come from me. Like I said, I don't want to be her caregiver – I want to be her granddaughter.

As far as my work is concerned, it didn't take me long to realize that work has been a major stressor for me and I really don't want to know or even care to know what is happening there right now. That realization came the second I shut off my computer and my phone and boarded the plane.

The truth of the matter is, I really don't miss the life I left on May 20, 2019. I definitely miss certain things and certain people, but I don't miss all the chaos, stress, fights, panic attacks and anxiety. I don't miss the lies, the feeling of being pulled in all different directions, being mad all the time, feeling used, taken advantage of and I don't miss being taken for granted. I have no problem saying what I don't want, but at the halfway point of my journey, I don't really know what I want or how I am going to get it.

Enough therapeutic journaling for now. My lodging tonight is at the Casa Rural Piedras Blancas, a simple rural home with nice basic rooms. I had read this village has a bird sanctuary/lagoon so, after freshening up, I went out in search of it. Unfortunately, it was pretty lackluster so I opted for an orange smoothie at a local café. I think what makes El Burgo Ranero more famous than the bird sanctuary are the large nests that sit atop the old church tower and the long-legged storks that stand watch over them.

After exploring my surroundings and a bit of relaxation, I grabbed some cheese and crackers and, of course, a Coke Zero and headed back to my room for the night. I spent some time in a video chat with my mom to provide her with a daily update and a virtual tour of my room and, after hanging up, I realized if it weren't for these calls, most of my days now would be spent in silence and I am perfectly okay with that. This is exactly where I need to be right now.

CHAPTER 21
June 9, 2019: El Burgo Ranero to Mansilla de las Mulas – 19 km

In kilometers, today was a short day but, in my reality, it seemed very long. The guidebook warned of a walk with little shade from the sun and of the lack of places to stop. In fact, the first and only real potential stop was 13 km away from where I started this morning. The first three hours were spent on a track paralleling a road with corn fields on either side so, again, there were no real distractions to take me away from the thoughts that popped into my head.

Well, there was one. The painful distraction of my feet. And when I say feet, I basically just mean a few of my toes. More specifically the two pinky toes and an infected toe that is now sporting a multi-colored nail. I had contemplated packing my sandals but I honestly thought I could walk the short 19 km in my trail runners. What was I thinking? Because of all the discomfort, I chose to barrel through the day just to get it over with. Didn't I do this a while back and then made a vow I would take better care of my feet? Reverting back to old behaviors seems to be the story of my life. Even through the agony of it, I can still find humour.

Walking right past a very small rest area earlier on in the day, I continued to struggle through the three hours it took to get to Reliegos for the only break I would take on the Camino trail. A very small village that sits at the junction of three Roman roads, the Via Trajana, the Real Camino Frances and a path from Leon. With the reward of my sandals dangling in front of me, I hobbled the remaining 6 km to Mansilla de las Mulas.

I arrived at 11:30 am and, immediately after retrieving my luggage, I went up to my room and gave my barking dogs a good rest. Feeling better, I then slipped on my sandals and ventured off to explore what Mansilla de las Mulas had to offer and it definitely didn't disappoint.

Three monuments still around from the medieval era are the bridge, one of the four original gates into the city and what still remains of the fortress walls. I walked past the bridge and found myself in the older part of town where the well-preserved streets allowed me to walk alongside the old fortress walls that once stood tall and strong. I can't even fathom how long it took to erect these massive barriers of stone. The craftmanship is amazing. Realizing I could get a better picture if I moved to the other side of the wall, I went off the path and found myself between the river and the medieval monument itself. And, for a split second, a frightful thought came to me. "I could be mugged, raped or killed on this side of the wall and nobody would even know."

The thought left my mind as fast as it had entered it, but what remained was the fact that this was the first time throughout this entire trip where I have felt vulnerable. I wasn't afraid or concerned that those things would actually happen to me because I have felt extremely safe this whole journey, but the thought was still there. As a woman travelling this Camino alone, there are a lot of things that could happen or, at least, is a common fear for solo females to have. I feel I have been taking the necessary precautions like keeping my money and important documents in a money belt or fanny pack and I have the added safety of my own private accommodations so, overall, I have been feeling extremely safe and have actually come to trust my fellow pilgrims. There is, no doubt, a sense of community and belonging on this path and I feel

Colleen Davis

the majority of the people on the Camino respect it enough to avoid doing anything that would tarnish the meaning behind it all. I am not saying that unfortunate things don't happen on the Camino and, probably, a good percentage of those things happen to women travelling alone, I am just saying that so far, I have felt very safe.

I then walked to the third monument still standing today, the Concepcion Gate which is still almost completely preserved. Again, I don't pretend to know anything about history and am actually in awe of the people I walk with who do. When I am with them, they share their knowledge but, most of the time, I just admire what I am looking at and then when I have WiFi, I google it. I was so intrigued by this small town that I did look a few things up and found that the Battle of Mansilla de las Mulas was held on December 30, 1808 and what I had walked on and through, and what I touched, took pictures of and admired, represents so much more than what my eyes could see.

After returning from my walkabout through the village, I went back to my room which is at the Albergueria del Camino. A small rural home that has been converted into a hotel. I retrieved my journal, found a nice quiet seat in the hotel's outside garden/dining area, ordered a café con leche and began writing my day's thoughts down on paper.

I mentioned that although today was only 19 km, it seemed very long. Partly because of my feet but also partly because I was back in my head. The irony is that at some point during today's walk I looked down and saw a rock with "think less" painted on it. I was going to take a picture of it as a reminder to myself but there was also bird poop on it making it a lot less photogenic.

How does one "think less" while walking the Meseta – the mental stage of this Camino? My mind takes me back to the train that

154

brought me to Saint-Jean-Pied-de-Port and the father and daughter who said they were doing the "best of the Camino" and totally skipping this section. No matter how many times I walk this Camino, and I will walk it again, I will never skip this part. Sure, it can be monotonous, arduous and at times somewhat boring. The weather can be brutal and the long stretches of total silence can become wearing on some people and, even though I write about how thought provoking this section is, I am finding peace, beauty and contentment in every part of this Camino, including the Meseta. It may sound weird, but I am finding this experience to be an up and down emotional roller coaster but not in a bad way, in a therapeutic, make you think kind of way.

The thoughts that have come up for me today, besides those that always seem to be coming up, are centered around the people I have met along the way. I got off that train in Saint-Jean-Pied-de-Port with a group of travellers with the same agenda – to spend the night there and then start walking the Camino Frances the very next day. Most of us started this journey together and, for the first two weeks we pretty much saw one another on a daily basis. Some took a rest day in Pamplona and others in Burgos, but somewhere along the Way, we would eventually find one another again. We would bump into each other at the end of the day, maybe share a drink and a few laughs and, some of us would even explore the town together all while making wonderful memories with total strangers. Then, all of a sudden, everyone was gone. I have spent most of my days on the Meseta alone, eating alone, exploring alone and just being alone. No David, Adam, Mike, Jack, Kim, Emily, Scott, Rachel or Cameron. Where did they all go?

I spoke with a man from Belgium while taking my break today and then a couple of women from Texas along the trail, but the conversations have been really short and that's fine. I am not saying any of this out of loneliness as I totally believe this is my Camino's way of telling me to focus. I seriously didn't come here on a "vacation." It was a much-needed leave of absence from my life and I have to be okay with the fact that this is how my Camino needs to look like today. I didn't come here to find friends, although, if I did that would be wonderful. I came here to find myself.

The first part of this journey has definitely been physical, but maybe it was more than just physically challenging due to the terrain I have walked on. Maybe it is also supposed to represent the physical part of my transformation into becoming my authentic self. Now there is a thought-provoking paragraph.

I would like to think that those people I met during the first two weeks represented different aspects of myself that I have lost. Most of these people have brought out my fun side. The part of me that loves to laugh, make others laugh and just live a little lighter. Then, there were those who brought out my caring and nurturing side. The part of me that gives just out of the kindness of my heart without expectations, even if it was just supplying a bandage to cover up a blister. With a few of them I found my vulnerable side, which has become really hard for me to be. Being vulnerable means having the ability to trust someone and that is something I have, unquestionably, lost. Since being here, I have shared very personal stories and experiences with the understanding, or trust, that there are no judgments and, if there have been any, accepting that those judgments come from their baggage and not mine. I, personally, have held no judgments on anything I have seen or heard. I honestly believe everyone here is exactly where they need to be and that what they are experiencing is happening for their very own specific reason.

I have felt no stress and no need to control situations. I am trying to accept what is happening on a daily basis as something that is supposed to be happening and I find when I do show some resistance or form of expectation, my Camino throws me a curve ball.

I am, by no means, saying I have found all the answers out here on the Meseta because I definitely haven't. What I am saying is that I have seen signs of the "old me" thanks to the people who have been placed along my path, so I have to believe they have come into my life for a specific reason and now they are gone. I feel the Camino is now guiding me into the next phase, the emotional and mental phase, and it is telling me that it needs to be done alone and, for the most part, in silent contemplation. I just wish with this silence came answers but, then again, maybe part of this lesson is to learn patience. Am I foolish to think that I can be transformed in thirty-nine days?

Here is another thought. Today, I passed by many symbols representing death. From the beautifully gated cemeteries to the various designs of the crosses that have been erected and strategically placed in honour of those peregrinos lost on the Way, these shrines seemed to be everywhere. It was so prevalent, that when I got settled into my room, I looked up the significance of the "roadside" crosses.

It was actually the Spanish who brought the tradition of "descansos" or "place of rest" to North America. While reading, the words that kept jumping off the page were "death," "mourning" and "place of healing." Am I to take this as a sign I need to mourn the loss or death of the person I was before May 20, 2019? Let that part of me rest in peace somewhere here on the Camino? Even though that pre-May 20, 2019, version of myself was lost, flawed, confused, scared, anxious, angry, numb and disconnected, she either represented a product of the situation around her or obtained those coats of armor in order to protect and get her through yet another stage in her life. Do I need to mourn the loss of her and begin the healing? Do I simply recognize that she did the best she could, let go and just move forward? These have been my thoughts and questions today – pretty deep huh. This is the magic and the curse of the Meseta.

As much as I find it very therapeutic to journal and put on paper these thoughts, feelings and questions, I want to end the day by going back to the staggering amount of history I have been witness to, especially today. Mansilla de las Mulas, which was originally called Manxilla by Picaud, was founded sometime before 1188, it played a role in the Napoleonic Wars, among others, and every step you take in this small town is an exemplary example of the medieval fortification used to allow for this place to still look the way it does after so much time and so much destruction. I may have come on this journey with the idea of soul searching and to, hopefully, find myself, but this journey is providing me with more than I had ever expected. I guess I was just so focused on the reason behind coming here that I didn't look past that to see everything else that would come with it. I will never forget how lucky I am to be afforded this opportunity.

Plus – I think I soaked my feet in an old chamber pot tonight.

CHAPTER 22
June 10, 2019: Mansilla de las Mulas to Leon – 20 km

Today's scenery was a hodgepodge of earth tracks and fields to pavement and highways. Even though a lot of the day was spent either on a dirt path beside the highway or walking on the shoulder of the highway itself, there was still a lot of beautiful things to see. I am madly in love with the bridges here so it is always a treat when I get to see or walk over one.

Thanks to a temporary pilgrim footbridge constructed in the village of Puente de Villarente, I was able to capture some amazing pictures of a beautiful medieval bridge that spans across the, once raging, Porma River. I think it originally had seventeen arches but current construction has added three more. Either way, this magnificent structure will be the longest bridge I see on this journey and, hopefully soon this footbridge will be lifted and pilgrims will, once again, walk over this impressive structure rather than beside it.

The peaceful paths and quaint villages were replaced with busier roads and then, after reaching the top of what was a gradual ascent, I got my first glance of the sprawling city of Leon. In the distance, I could also see mountain ranges which serve as a reminder I will soon be leaving the Meseta and the "emotional" stage and making my transition into the "spiritual" stage. Crossing over the highway via a large blue pedestrian walkway, the Camino trail worked its way through the urban areas of Leon and into old town.

Again, I have to say I did not experience the three different stages of personal growth along my Camino pilgrimage in the order that every single website will state. Whenever I wrote those words in my journal, I
159

was basically just reiterating the "staged" approach to the Camino Frances. Of course, the first part was extremely physical, but it was also extremely emotional for me. And, I experienced spiritual moments throughout my entire journey. I found that when I finally did let go of the "three stage" expectation, along with all the other expectations I went in with, I was able to not only recognize what was being triggered in me, but I was also able to feel everything that was coming up as well. And, letting go of it all gave me the opportunity to enjoy and be present for everything and anything.

I had left Mansilla de las Mulas at 6:30 this morning and, even though I passed through several small villages, I didn't really take many breaks. My feet were actually feeling great and I really just felt like walking. It took me four and a half hours to get to Leon and, luckily, my room was ready for me when I arrived.

I am staying at the Hostal Quevedo, a very impressive little hotel located on a pedestrianized street right on the Camino route. My balcony even overlooks the Quevedo Park, a beautiful little park that I made sure to visit.

I can't remember exactly what time it was, but at some point during the day I began craving a McDonald's strawberry milkshake and I told myself that if I came across a McDonald's while searching for my hotel I was going to stop and buy one. I haven't seen a McDonald's in three weeks and really, considering my surroundings, was not anticipating actually seeing one at all. Well, what do I pass this morning coming into Leon? A McDonald's! I convinced myself it was just way too early in the morning for a shake and that maybe I would come back later to scratch that itch. But, now that I know where my hotel is, the one and only McDonald's is just way too far away, so I won't be getting that milkshake.

It was also along the bank of the Bernesga River while entering Leon that I stopped and talked to a couple of German fellows who are completing the Camino on horseback. They are also documenting their journey for a documentary to be released at a later time. I have heard about them, have seen their horse trailers parked at remote farmhouses along the Way and have, on several occasions, avoided stepping in the offerings their horses have left behind on the trail, but I haven't had the opportunity to meet them until today so I stopped and chatted for a bit before wishing them and their horses a "Buen Camino." As they prepared themselves to leave the city, both dressed up like knights with their horses draped in caparisons, I started thinking how corny it all looked. So much for me being nonjudgmental. I have worked in the television industry so I can totally understand how "entertaining" everything needs to look but for me, personally, that whole visual seemed to take away from the depth and meaning behind the actual Camino itself. Like, what purpose was the colorful attire actually serving besides just being visually appealing? Who knows, maybe one day I will have the opportunity to see this documentary and my questions will be answered.

The former Capital of the Kingdom of Leon is a very beautiful city and, because I arrived early, I had lots of time to explore. The first thing I did was find the Cathedral, which wasn't hard to do considering it is massive. By the time I arrived at its doors, the Cathedral was only going to be open for another thirty minutes so I missed out on seeing all the stained-glass windows it is famous for. I then went over to the hotel Parador of San Marcos. Construction on this former pilgrim's hospital began in the 16th century and is currently in the middle of being renovated so I didn't get a chance to go in there either. Instead of being disappointed, I just turned around and continued my exploration of this awe-inspiring city. In the old quarter, I got to see a large part of a medieval wall and some remains of the original Roman Wall that once surrounded the city.

Finding my way to a small café, I purchased a café con leche and a white chocolate pastry. My brother specifically said I needed to try everything, so that's what I am going to do. Sitting at one of the cafés outside tables, I dove into that pastry and enjoyed a few moments of people watching. I was soon joined by Ben from Germany, a gentleman I have seen off and on for the last few days. We are usually one of the first ones to start walking in the mornings and share a cordial "Buen Camino" before carrying on. I have also seen him at various rest stops or cafés but have never really shared a conversation with him before today. He started his journey three months ago right from his house somewhere in Germany. He literally walked out his front door and just kept going.

As we sat and watched pilgrims make their way into the city and tourists soaking up all of Leon's history and appeal, Ben and I discussed how neither one of us were really missing much from home. One attribute we each share is the fact we are two very responsible people who seem to look after everyone else's needs, ignoring our own in the process. He mentioned how anxious he was back at home and that now he feels so much better, both mentally and physically.

He was surprised to hear how I can feel that same difference after only three weeks. I then explained that the fact I can feel this change after only three weeks is proof to how desperately it needed to happen. To be honest, I felt a difference after three hours of being away from my environment. Sometimes a person needs to be instantly plucked from the situation they are in and removed from the insanity so they can open their eyes and actually see what is beyond the chaos that had been suffocating them. I needed to see beyond what my reality was becoming and I am very grateful I had the financial capability plus an understanding husband and boss for allowing me the time to do this. To be clear, I would have done it anyway because I was heading down a path that was starting to scare me. It is just nice to know that I have the backing of my spouse and the person who signs my pay cheques.

After saying goodbye to Ben, I took a nice walk through the park across from my hotel. I then purchased some food to eat up in my room and am now enjoying the ambiance and view from my balcony. I have soaked my feet in yet another bidet because that's just what needs to be done along this Camino of mine. I will work on a couple of blisters, do some shin splint stretches and call it a night. Tomorrow is my last 31 km day on the trail and I want to be refreshed and renewed for the long walk.

CHAPTER 23
June 11, 2019: Leon to Hospital de Orbigo – 31 km

My body was very tired today. My hips, legs and feet just felt so worn out and sore and it wasn't like I was struggling on the trail because I wasn't. It was just an achy body kind of day. Considering what I am putting my body through on a daily basis, I can do nothing more than be understanding. If my body feels like retaliating and bellyaching every once in a while, I am going to let it.

I walked through a lot of little towns and villages today, which makes long days like this just a little bit more enjoyable. I am starting to notice a change in scenery and terrain as the landscape gets a little bit more undulating and the palette starts showing splashes of green. Still plenty of pavement and straight tracks that continue to hug the main road, but all with the absence of vehicles, which is very nice.

I chose to pause the start of my day until I saw other pilgrims pass by my window because I had read that the signs or markers leaving Leon would be a little more difficult to follow and I didn't want to get lost, a legitimate concern for someone travelling solo. Getting a glance at my unsuspecting leaders, I put my jacket, shoes and daypack on, took a selfie to, once again, prove I am actually here, grabbed my walking stick and proceeded out the door.

It was such a gorgeous walk out of Leon. The fine line between twilight and dawn had not yet broke and, although the streetlights were still on and illuminating the light blue sky, I knew it was just a matter of time before they would turn off, marking the start of another normal day in the city. As much as I don't consider myself a morning person, it really is the most peaceful time of the day. And what made it even more peaceful was the fact I had these two pilgrims in front of me leading the way, giving me the opportunity to let my guard down enough to enjoy the view.

I wasn't expecting the people I was following to stop for breakfast 5 km in and because I wasn't ready to stop, I soon found myself in the "lead" with others now following me. It was true, at times the path was not as well marked as it could have been and I felt I really had to pay attention to my surroundings but it was all good. Early on, I was given the option to take an alternate route that led away from the road, was quieter and, apparently, supposed to be more beautiful but it also tacked on a few extra kilometers to an already 31 km day. I chose to stay on the direct path and not because it was shorter but because it followed the original Way of St. James and I want to walk as much of the original path as possible. So, I continued to follow the road for most of the day and even took the opportunity to put my mark on the wall of an underpass just as others before me had done. A simple name and year to mark my Camino existence in the hopes that one day I will see it again.

If I was a religious person or a history buff, I would have had several reasons to stop and explore the different places I passed, but I am neither, so I would admire the things I could see along the trail and then keep moving. At one point I thought I had stepped foot on the movie set of the Hobbit thanks to all the bodegas I found myself curiously admiring. These bodegas, or underground wine cellars, are literally earthen mound type structures built right into the rolling hillsides.

I met two sisters from Michigan today. I had seen them a few days ago on the trail and, at that time, what stood out for me was that they both looked really young and that one was walking as if at some point in her life she had suffered a stroke. Well, it turns out she did have a stroke a few days after she was born and whatever current disabilities she may have, she definitely doesn't allow them to stop her from doing anything and everything. One had just finished her Theology studies abroad and the other had flown out from Michigan so that they could experience the Camino together. Now that the one is done her studies; she is taking this time on the Camino to decide whether or not she actually wants to continue in the career path she has studied for. The other is here to find her authentic self. She feels she has lost herself in social media and all the pressures of society. She said she doesn't even know herself anymore. Sound familiar? Yup! Ironically, her phone died as soon as she met up with her sister in France and she says she doesn't miss it at all. Maybe it was her Camino giving her a sign. No "Maybes," her Camino was undoubtedly giving her a sign.

Now that it has been almost three years since I have completed my Camino and I can see the progress I have made in my resolution to change certain aspects of my life that desperately needed to be changed and am just as aware of the lack of progress in others, I am curious to know how my fellow pilgrims are doing with any revelations they may have made on their journey. Any conclusions or dedications for change. I met a lot of interesting people with a lot of very unique stories and life questions. I also met a lot of people with very similar issues as mine that they were struggling with and I am just wondering if they vowed to go home and make changes and then actually went home and applied those changes.

To be clear, I am not judging myself for the "lack of progress" at all. I am very proud of myself for the personal work I did both on the

Camino as well as post Camino. I can now recognize when I am falling into the same patterns that weren't serving me then and still aren't serving me now and yet, I understand that Rome wasn't built in a day. There are a couple of people from my time on the Camino who I try to keep in touch with but there are many more I met who shared their angst, struggles, issues and questions with me who I wonder about and hope they found their peace just as I am slowly finding mine.

A couple of Random Acts of Kindness were also bestowed upon me today. Gestures I am not quite familiar with being on the receiving end of. This morning, I stopped at a quaint café for my daily glass of orange juice and was given a tortilla at no extra charge. This was my first tortilla of the entire trip and, boy, was it ever good. It was like a little piece of heaven masquerading as an egg and hash brown pie. Later, Dolores, the Proprietor of the establishment I am staying at this evening, saw me sitting in the garden and brought me a coffee and a piece of sweet bread to enjoy while I relaxed. It really is the little things that provide the most pleasure.

I have absolutely no internet connection out here in this beautiful garden and I really don't care. During our time together, the two sisters told me that, sometimes when they reach their town or village early in the day, they get bored. I can honestly say I haven't been bored once throughout this entire trip. Maybe it's the age difference or the importance placed on the social aspect of the journey. I read that a lot while doing my research on the Camino that there is a large social component to it. Makes sense considering that most pilgrims stay in municipal albergues and hostels, which would make it pretty difficult to not be somewhat social. I am quite content being exactly where I am right now which is in Hospital de Orbigo at Casa Rural Nuestra Senora de Lourdes just sitting out back in Dolores' garden filled with cherry trees, a fish pond, a lot of old relics hanging from the fences, a palm tree and my clothes hanging from the line. It is just me right now and I believe I will be the only pilgrim staying here tonight as well.

It feels very weird being called a "pilgrim". As I walked today, I tried to imagine what it would have been like a thousand years ago when there were no modern roads, traffic circles, hotels or yellow arrows marking the Way. Back when the stone walls, arches and castles stood tall and the magnificent bridges were new. And, back when there were no quaint little cafés to stop at to rest your feet or a supermercado to walk into and grab a desperately needed bottle of water or, in my case, a chocolate bar. A lot has changed in the years since St. James did this pilgrimage but those changes don't negate the fact, I am actually still a pilgrim and am partaking in my own type of pilgrimage. A sentence I never thought would pertain to me and a quest I never would have believed I would be taking but, here I am.

So, as I sit here in this magical garden listening to the faint brays of a donkey and wondering if that particular little guy belongs to the family I saw travelling with their four children and two donkeys, my mind continues to jump from one thought to another. The one that seems to be in the forefront right now is the car accident and the reactions made by a few people close to me.

I know they don't believe I was injured to the extent that I actually was in that accident and I also know some feel I received too much money as compensation for my non-existent injuries even though they have no idea how much I was awarded. One remark that stands out is, "Whatever she got was too much." This could only mean that even if the settlement awarded me was in the amount of fifty dollars for a high-speed rollover that caused extensive and unrepairable damage to the vehicle, in their mind, it was fifty dollars too much. That's pretty sad.

The amount I received is not important and something I don't dwell on because, in the end, I will never feel it was enough to compensate for the pain I will endure for the rest of my life, but it is, among other things, a contributing factor to me being able to sit here in this garden. That, and all the hard work I personally did for the past four years. The physiotherapy, the chiropractic treatments, the special exercises I had to do on a daily basis, the surgery, the recovery regimen after the surgery and especially the drive and determination I had to not allow any of those road blocks stop me from doing this pilgrimage or any other thing I want to accomplish in life.

I may say that if it wasn't for the accident or the money from the accident, I wouldn't be on this pilgrimage but that's not necessarily true. This is a journey that was desperately needed. And, if it wasn't in Spain, I truly believe it would have happened somewhere else. If I am being totally honest with myself, I have been lost for a very long time. My heart, my soul and my core beliefs and values have never changed, but living a life based on the labels and roles I was given by others only stunted me from finding my authentic self. Sure, that little eleven-year-old girl who stood in between her father and mother with the intent of saving her mom from being further slapped in the face by attempting to push her dad out the bathroom door while yelling at him to stop, not only felt she had the power to save her mom but could now save everyone else in the house from the abuse and chaos. I felt like I could save everyone from everything. That was a role I played and the burden I carried for a very long time. Some would say I still do. Wife, mother, single mother, rescuer, caretaker, party planner, advocate etc. etc. All roles. Roles I was given, I chose, I accepted, I earned and I excelled at. The other roles such as liar, victim, villain, cheater and fraudster have all been unjustifiably placed on me by people who claim to know, love, care and appreciate me. What have I done to them to have this judgement placed on me? Is it me? Is it their own insecurities? Is it jealousy?

All I know is that I have never felt more vulnerable than I have since the accident and it's because, since the accident, I have needed people's help and I am not used to that feeling. I am used to being the person who is there for those who are in a vulnerable state. And, I feel, because of my vulnerability or "role reversal" situation I find myself in, I am now seeing how people really feel about me, whether it's based on their own issues or on how they actually feel about me, it doesn't really matter. What matters is that I have had to absorb all of that toxicity while also trying to juggle and deal with my own shit. What ended up happening was that everything just came crashing down. So, again, even though the money took away the stress of just picking up and leaving for a month, I honestly believe it was only a matter of time before I would have taken that temporary leave of absence from my life with or without that financial security.

Selfish. Now there is a word I never thought I would call myself, or a label I would so proudly wear but, after fifty-one years, I have finally learned it is okay to be selfish and, sometimes, it's extremely necessary. I have spent my whole life focusing on other people's needs and wants. I have given and given and given to others and now it is time to take care of myself. To take care of my emotional, spiritual and physical well-being.

I am scared shitless that I am going to go home and jump right back into the life I no longer want to live. That would be easy, but as I write this, I truly hope it will become impossible to do. That the strength, wisdom, courage and insight I gain on this Camino will prevent me from going backwards. As for what others feel or think about me, that will just have to be their shit and that's where it will stay, with them. What they think or feel does not define who I am. What they believe does not have to control me. I have given people my power for too long and I think it's about time that I took it back.

Well, that was therapeutic. I honestly didn't think I would be sitting out here for as long as I have and I also didn't think I had that much to write about today. I did look back on some of the pictures I took today and the one that really caught my eye was the selfie I took first thing this morning. It's really the first time I have taken notice of the physical transformation that is happening with my body. I guess I just haven't given it any thought, but it only makes sense there would be some changes and possible weight loss. That wasn't the only thing I noticed in the picture. I also look happy. Happy, content and healthy. And, not just physically healthy. I think maybe I can see some mental clarity and newfound joy in my eyes as well.

The most impressive feature, for me, here in Hospital de Orbigo is the massive medieval bridge. An extremely long and well-preserved stone bridge that has a very interesting story behind it. In 1434, the Leonese knight, Suero de Quinones invited other knights from all over Europe to joust him on top of the bridge to prove that he was worthy of the love of his lady. He won every battle for a month breaking three hundred lances by the end of it.

I can't really say I thought much about this story as I walked across the bridge itself. As a matter of fact, I must have walked across that bridge and back at least five times just to take in as much of it as I could. It is absolutely gorgeous. The river it once crossed has since dried up allowing me the opportunity to walk under it and take in even more of this simple yet magnetic structure. And the photo ops were amazing!

I may decide to take another walk before retiring to my room, I may not. I may just fold my laundry, find some form of dinner and call it a night. For now, I think I will just close up this journal, close my eyes and give everything a bit of a break for a while.

CHAPTER 24
June 12, 2019: Hospital de Orbigo to Astorga– 17 km

Today seemed to really fly by, which, now that the end of this walk is in sight, is not what I want my remaining days to do.

I started this morning sitting alone in the common breakfast area having, what I thought, was an included meal. It was only after I was handed the one piece of toast, one package of marmalade, a muffin (with butter, which is a hot commodity on the Camino) and a coffee that I was told it was actually going to cost €3. Because of the generous amount of hospitality I have been shown here, I had absolutely no problem paying that and a bit more for breakfast. I ate most of it but then stuffed the muffin and butter in my daypack for later and said my goodbyes to Dolores and Hospital de Orbigo.

Almost immediately after departing, I met up with another solo female walker who was also just leaving her albergue so we decided to walk together and we remained walking together for the whole day.

Shortly after leaving Hospital de Orbigo, we were given the option of either going to the left for an easy walk along a path that followed the main road or going to the right which would add some distance to the day but steer us away from the traffic noise. We chose to stay to the left and, again, it wasn't because it was shorter. It's because I want to stay as true to the original path as much as possible.

The landscape is also, noticeably, continuing to change. The fairly level grounds are starting to show some rise and falls and the scenery is changing from the wheat-coloured plains of the Meseta to the arrival of those distant mountains (Montes de Leon) I will soon have to maneuver my way across. The various shades of green adorning the trees that are starting to appear again are also a welcoming sight.

This section of my Camino took four hours to do; passing a few small villages along the way. A small statue of St. James at the entrance to one and a large stone cross commemorating a bishop are just a few of the monuments and statues I continue to walk by or stop to admire and reflect at. There are so many things I have seen that truly hold the spirit of the Camino; from the largest statue or monument I have come across to the smallest picture hanging silently from a tree. We stopped at one of these small villages for a quick coffee but that was the only stop we made. And, I don't believe it was the lack of kilometers that made the day go by so fast, but the endless conversation that just seemed to flow with this woman I had met this morning.

Her name was Helene and she is from Stockholm, Sweden. Listening to her talk was like hearing my own story being spoken out loud. Her life is extremely stressful, she doesn't know what she wants but knows she is in desperate need of a change. She feels she has lost herself somewhere in the chaos and doesn't really know how to "feel anymore." Boy, does that ever resonate with me. She is also afraid that when she goes home, she will just automatically get dropped right back into the thick of things. We definitely had a lot in common and had a lot to talk about. And, it's not like I was glad to hear that other people out there are struggling just as much as I am. That they are feeling the same types of emotions or lack of emotions and living with the same angsts as I am but, on the other hand, it is such a relief to know I am not alone. It is so validating! Hearing that other people have the same thoughts I have been having kind of takes the craziness of it all away. It's not only validating but it is somewhat comforting to know I am surrounded by people who are searching, questioning, processing, doubting and fearing the same things that I am. I don't even know if any of that made sense but it just felt right to put it to paper.

I strongly believe my Camino is bringing these people to me and I welcome them all in. Yes, I came here to be alone and I still feel that way but the few people my Camino does put in my path feel like extensions of myself and I am learning something from each and every one of them. They arrive, they walk for a while and when they leave, they leave behind something I was looking for. Maybe I am transitioning into the spiritual part of my journey, I don't know, but whatever it is, I am just going to go with the flow.

Arriving into Astorga as early as I did allowed me the opportunity to explore the city and take in its enormous amount of history. The first place I visited was the Roman Museum of Astorga. Just making the trip to the museum, itself, was a treat for the eyeballs. I had to pass through the Plaza Mayor, lined with outdoor cafés and restaurants, and then towards Astorga's architecturally gorgeous City Hall, a grand building built in 1704. The animated clock tower, the many bells and all the statues chiseled on its façade were absolutely breathtaking. The museum, unfortunately, was just okay for me. Considering I have literally walked on the remains of actual Roman roads and have passed by ancient relics and ruins from the Roman era, I entered the museum with too high of an expectation.

Built around actual ruins, the museum has two floors to it. Upstairs had the typical Roman artifacts such as jewelry, plates and various fragments of items found during excavations and on the main floor they had a twelve-minute video that I, literally, had to power through. The entire video was spoken in Spanish with English subtitles and it was clear that some things either can't or shouldn't be translated because it was really hard to understand. Apparently, if you book ahead, they have guided tours of places not open to the public such as the thermal baths, ergastula (the buildings used to hold slaves) and the Roman sewers. That probably would have been more interesting, but I had just missed the last one for the day.

The two other monuments definitely worth seeing are the Episcopal Palace and the Cathedral which are practically right beside each other. Built between 1889 and 1913, the palace now serves as a museum of religious art called *Museo de los Caminos*, dedicated to the Way of Santiago. The palace/museum was closed when I walked by so I paid the extra few euro and did an audio tour of the Cathedral instead. Like most of the churches I have visited along the Camino, this one was adorned with architectural masterpieces from beginning to end. The only difference being is that this one is on a much grander scale than the others. This particular cathedral is massive. The meaning behind all the grandeur is wasted on me because I don't understand its religious significance but, I am definitely impressed and in awe of the construction, detail, beauty and history of it all. Personally though, I feel it is just a little too much.

What I found the most interesting and exciting was what I stumbled upon while on the hunt for my "tacky tourist" gift.

My "tacky tourist" gift explained. When my nephew and child were young, I would buy them little gifts from all the places I had travelled to. Mostly from the western states of the US. I would purchase them little license plates or mugs with their names written on them or hats and t-shirts that bore the name of the city I was in.

It was in Reno, Nevada, where I decided instead of buying something for others, I would, instead, buy myself a little souvenir. I picked out the cheapest and tackiest item I could find which, at that time, was a ninety-nine-cent tiny ceramic mug with "Reno" written on it along with their slogan of being "the Biggest little City in the World." The tiny little mug, itself, held a handful of toothpicks and I thought it was the perfect gift to start my collection. Well, these little mugs are no longer ninety-nine cents and they are becoming a lot harder to find, so I have had to make a few adjustments. If I can't find a mug, I will settle for a shot glass and if I can't find a mug or a shot glass with toothpicks, then I grab toothpicks from a restaurant or pub within the same city.

I consider myself extremely lucky that my place of employment allows me the opportunity to travel but, once again, it is usually within the Western part of Canada and the US so my collection is pretty modest. I decided on this Camino that it just wouldn't be feasible to collect these little trinkets from every town, village or city I walked through because, first off, there were a lot of places I walked through and, secondly, because of the lack of space I had to carry them all in. I chose to only purchase them at the larger cities and, even then, it was dependent on how much room I had in my suitcase. The more items I left behind on the Camino became the space I used to store my treasures.

It was during a modern excavation in Astorga that a third of a private home dating back to the end of the 1st century A.D. and the first half of the 4th century was uncovered. Experts believe the dwelling belonged to a wealthy family because of all the additions that had been added on to the home. I didn't have to go to a museum or pay anything to see this because it was literally "just there" on the side of the street.

While walking to a gift shop, I noticed that something had been roped off and then I saw small pedestrian bridges leading up and over the remains. Finally, I stopped at a sign that explained exactly what I was looking at and I still had a hard time believing what I was actually seeing.

These are the moments that are taking my breath away and these are the situations I am finding myself in that make me want to pinch myself just to make sure it's not all just a dream. These are the added little gems reminding me to take in every minute and every second of this journey. If I hadn't been consciously doing just that, I could have easily just walked by this magnificent piece of history without even knowing.

Along with purchasing my tacky tourist gift, I also bought some essential items my guidebook has advised to purchase because of the lack of services that will be available for the next couple of days. I am now back in my room which is at the Hostal A Coruna. The building is just a short walk from the historical center and the area it is located in reminds me of an older part of Vancouver I drive through whenever I am there visiting Kelly. The room is spacious, simple and provides me with all the necessities and amenities needed to prepare for tomorrow.

Having looked ahead in my guidebook, the route is supposed to start changing dramatically. Tomorrow is to be an entire day spent gradually ascending into an obvious change of scenery. This could only mean one thing. I have survived, conquered and am now phasing out of the Meseta.

Now that this stage is pretty much over, I can say it was certainly more taxing on the mind than any other section so far, but it was far from unpleasant. I guess I came into this with a preconceived notion of what the Meseta would be like and I was pleasantly surprised by what it actually turned out to be. And, although I am looking forward to the change of scenery as I begin my Montes de Leon climb, it all just continues to be a reminder that I am entering the last stage of my Camino and I am so not ready for it to be over.

Another preconceived notion I had was that I would come out of the Meseta a little bit more enlightened. That all my questions would be answered, all my doubts and fears would be dealt with and that all my frustrations would be gone. That is not the case. I am still finding it very hard to use the time I am walking alone to do the work I think I "should" be doing. I wake up in the morning with full and good intentions of picking out one issue I have, one problem or one of the reasons that has brought me here and then analyze it, dissect it, and eventually come to an "aha" moment. That moment of realization and answers. That moment of knowing what needs to be done in order for me to gain some peace. But then I start walking and I find myself distracted by so many things or by nothing at all. The sound of my sneakers as they hit the gravel, the conversation being had by the people walking ahead of me, the immense visual beauty surrounding me, the feel of the rain, or wind or sun on my face, the overwhelming sense of gratitude that takes over as I look around in disbelief that I am actually here. The number of feelings being had; feelings I haven't felt in a very long time. The total sense of calm that I don't want fading away by introducing an issue into my train of thought. Next thing I know, I have made it to my overnight destination and realize I haven't given any thought to my life back at home or any of the baggage I initially intended to unload.

I just have to trust in my Camino and trust in the fact that maybe I am spending each of those days exactly the way my Camino intended them to be spent. And, knowing I can't slow down time, I will continue to take in every second and every moment of this gift I have been given and that answers will present themselves in their own time. The finish line is just coming way sooner than I want it to.

CHAPTER 25
June 13, 2019: Astorga to Rabenal Del Camino – 21 km

What an incredible day! I had the worst night's sleep last night and, because today was supposed to be a continuous climb, I was expecting it to be slow moving and quiet. The walk out of Astorga was just that. I then caught up to Lisa, who was part of the group I constantly saw in the beginning but then, later, lost on the trail. Lisa has been dealing with some really painful knee injuries which have forced her to slow it down and take it easy so, I slowed my pace and walked with her for a while. She caught me up on where the rest of the crew currently are and I was quite pleased to hear that Emily and Scott were not that far behind us.

The path leading out of Astorga was a comfortable one but, after walking for about an hour, it became progressively steeper and stayed that way for the rest of the day. It wasn't so much demanding as it was constant. Lisa and I eventually parted ways with a friendly "Buen Camino" and, because the villages were quite sparse and tiny, I didn't take my first break until I was 14 km into the walk. I then stopped at El Ganso, the last village I would come across before reaching my destination for the night, Rabenal Del Camino.

I stopped at a small restaurant tucked away in a convenient enough spot where I could enjoy my café con leche while watching pilgrims walk by. I found a spot on a long rectangular table outside of the building and took a well-deserved break.

As more people began to stop, I struck up a conversation with a gentleman named Jonas who is, apparently, some type of celebrity back in his home country. What struck me in the conversation was that we didn't spend much time talking about what he "does" but rather "who he is" and what brought him here.

This is something I found throughout my entire walk. I could have been talking to a bunch of celebrities, millionaires or maybe even royalty, but that just wasn't important or even something I looked out for or gave much thought to. We were all just people on a journey in search of something. Folks walk the Camino for a reason and it is definitely not to impress or boast about where they come from or what they do for a living. Of course, those questions were asked and answered, but there were deeper and more meaningful matters that had brought us all there. Whether it was to challenge ourselves physically, renew our faith in or find religion, take in the history or, like me, attempt to find one's self in whatever way that looks like.

Jonas had been diagnosed with ADHD and, because of that, he has used his celebrity status to focus on speaking out about it. He also shared that his young son is currently fighting cancer. One might ask why a father whose son is currently battling a life-threatening disease would be sitting at a café in the middle of Northern Spain sharing his story with me rather than being at home with his family and the answer is simple. It's probably for the same reason why a middle-aged woman whose husband just recently had a major heart attack and whose world back home is currently falling apart is sitting at a café in the middle of Northern Spain listening to his story. That's how important and necessary it is for the two of us to be here that we are prepared to eliminate ourselves from serious situations currently happening back home; situations that not only include us but affect us as well. If we can't find the strength to help ourselves then how are we going to be of any use to anyone else back at home.

He had such a compelling story and as intriguing as it was, something else was standing out for me. The first thing I had noticed about him was that he had a feather strategically placed in his buff and the reason I was struck by that was because, earlier today, I walked by another gentleman who had a feather tucked in his buff as well.

I was walking alone at the time when my attention was drawn to a man walking ahead of me. It wasn't so much that he was walking in front of me, it was the fact he was walking about ten feet off the path and not actually on it. He had only walked for a short time before I realized that what he was actually doing was getting off the path to take a break. Maybe have a drink of water, a snack, I really don't know, but he was taking off his backpack as I walked by. Still, none of that explains the reason why my attention was first drawn to this man. There was just something about the way he looked. He had the look of a gypsy, a free-spirited nomad and for a second, I had hoped our eyes would have met as I walked by so I could just say "Hi." Nothing more, just for the two of us to recognize we had seen each other, acknowledged one another's presence and then carried on with our lives.

So, as I sat enjoying my coffee and conversation with Jonas at this little café in a tiny village along the Camino, the intriguing man I had passed earlier on, not only caught up to me, but proceeded to join us at our table. Jonas seemed to be familiar with him and they exchanged pleasantries. Jonas even pointed to his feather and told the man he had specifically placed it there because he had previously seen this man's feather and thought it was cool. They shared a laugh and then Jonas and

I continued with our conversation. After a while, Jonas said his goodbyes and left.

The man's name was Dee Sunshine and, after introducing himself to me, he said he hadn't meant to eavesdrop but found what Jonas and I were talking about to be very interesting. I then did something I hadn't done this entire journey. I sat there for over two hours engaged in an entertaining, deep and very meaningful conversation with Dee. I sat there and watched as many of the people I had passed earlier on in the day walked by, including Emily and Scott and a few others I had started this adventure with. Some stopped for a quick bite to eat and a brief "Hello" and others simply smiled, waved and walked right on through.

Originally from Scotland, Dee had, at this point, been travelling for the past six months. This was his second time on the Camino in less than a year. He is a fifty-seven-year-old, self-proclaimed, gypsy (and I call him that with the outmost respect) who, at this stage in his life, has nothing more than ten boxes of possessions currently stored at his mom's house. He studies and practices the true art of yoga, tantric yoga, meditation and healing. As I sat there listening to his story, I realized that this man has absolutely no problem talking his truth with the occasional "fuck" and "cunt" thrown in for good measure.

He definitely had his own issues; as do we all, but I admired the way he owned his authentic self. He seemed very attuned to his wants and needs, giving no explanation or desire to explain or justify how he chooses to live his life, no apologies for the way he speaks and no thought to what others think about how he dresses. The attire he was wearing, which I thought was an eclectic mix and really wished I could pull off, were items he had picked up along the way. Articles others had left behind at various hostels.

His father had recently passed away leaving Dee with a bit of an inheritance so he was taking this time on the Camino to find the answers to what he should do with this money. Feeling like he has learned and gained so much knowledge and wisdom throughout his own journey, he thinks it may be time to share his talents and gifts with others. He just doesn't know what that looks like at this point.

At one point in our conversation, he asked if he could interview me for a project he is doing while on the Camino. His intentions are to ask a select number of people some questions regarding their reasons, expectations and experiences on the Way and then later either write a book or put something up on YouTube. He also said that "absolutely nothing at all could come of it" but I thought it was an interesting idea and was enjoying the conversation so I said "Sure."

Not only did we sit and talk for the better part of the afternoon, we then continued our conversation while walking the next 6 km to Rabenal Del Camino together. The climb continued and became gradually steeper the closer we got. It was no wonder, considering that Rabenal Del Camino represents the halfway point to the top of Irago Mountain, a legendary pass in the history of the Camino Frances. Dee admittedly walks at a slower pace than others but I knew my day would still end relatively early, so I didn't mind plus, I was enjoying the company. We came upon a clearing in the wooded section we had been travelling through, just before the steepest climb of the day, and decided stop, rest and admire a couple of falcons that were randomly on display. For a few euro you could even have your picture taken with them. I have been to several touristy places with this type of set up, but

I never would have expected to see this out in the middle of nowhere. Opportunity can definitely be had just about anywhere.

While on the trail together, Dee asked me if I knew what I wanted and I said "No, but I can definitely tell you what I don't want." His advice to me was to stop concentrating on the things I don't want because when I do, I am giving those negative thoughts energy and life. Not only will that continue to feed that energy into those things I no longer want in my life but it will continue to attract them as well.

Tomorrow marks the day I climb to the Iron Cross, which is a very significant part of the Camino. Dee's continued advice to me was to leave all the "don't wants" up there and to spend the rest of my Camino concentrating on the things I do want. Start giving them the life they deserve with the hope I will start attracting those things. He mentioned that he, too, journals and maybe every day when I journal, I could list three things I am grateful for.

As inspiring as his speech was and as motivated as I feel right now, all I can say is that I will try to make that my goal. I don't know if it will be one I will continue to follow but, for today, I am grateful for my feet for getting me to this point, my health for allowing me the opportunity to be here and I am especially grateful for meeting Dee.

We ended our time together in Rabanal Del Camino and marked our brief relationship with a selfie, a quick hug goodbye and the idea that if we see each other again, we do, and if we don't, then we are both content with having shared this moment together. He definitely left me with a lot to think about and a reminder that I still have so much more exploring to do when it comes to finding my authentic self. One thing I do know is that I want to be accepted for who I am, when I find out who that actually is, and not for what I can do for others. I want to care less about what people think about me and concentrate on living a simple and happy life. That may seem a bit broad but, for now, it's a start.

My room for the night is at the Hotel La Posada de Gaspar, a medieval building dating back to the 17th century and known to be a former pilgrim's hospital. The town is located at the halfway point of this mountain and has one main street. A street that either goes straight uphill or straight downhill depending on which direction you are heading in. My hotel is located on this main street at the far end of town, which only meant no matter where I decided to go this evening, I had a hill to climb on my return back. My room faces the street so every once in a while, I will open up the window and watch as people walk by.

Even though I decided to have a private room, I did enjoy being able to look out my window or sit on my deck and watch others walk by and this is something I will take into consideration for my next Camino. Because this was my first and I had no idea what I was walking into (pun intended) I didn't realize that some of my accommodations weren't necessarily going to be on the Camino itself and, at times, they would be extremely out of the way. As much as I wanted to be alone, there is still that basic desire to belong, to see a familiar face or share in something greater than us all and still feel like you are actually a part of it. I wanted to be on the Camino even when I was resting. I wanted to be able to walk down a street and know that the person I just passed carrying a walking stick, lugging a backpack or sporting bandages on their feet had just experienced the same type of day that I had. That they had just walked the same path as I had. Believe me, it doesn't take long to feel like a family and that connection is very important. I will probably continue to use a company to plan my next Camino, but I will be specific in saying I would like all my accommodations to be on or very close to the Camino trail

After cleaning up and taking care of my feet, I met Helene and we sat on a bench and talked while she waited for her dinner companions. I declined their invitation to join them, choosing to find something at a small market and taking it back up to my room. I did explore the village a bit, which meant walking up and down that hill several times, and that is because I find I crave walking, even after a long day of it. This adventure has so many wonderful and beautiful things to see and I just don't want to miss any of it, even if it means hills have to be climbed.

CHAPTER 26
June 14, 2019: Rabenal Del Camino to Molinaseca– 25 km

Happy fourth Birthday, Lukas. Lukas has done more for me in four short years than others have my entire life. He has brought me so much joy and has filled my cup on so many occasions. As much as I feared a devastating ache of missing him throughout this journey, I find I am actually doing okay. He was the hardest to say goodbye to and one of the first I want to see when I get back home but for now, I am okay. Just the thought of him makes me smile and that is enough.

Today, I am grateful for my walking stick for keeping me from falling, I am grateful for my spirit for choosing to walk this section which, for the most part, was downhill and very hard on my toe. It would have been so easy to opt out and take a cab, but then I wouldn't have had the experiences I had today. Finally, I am grateful for two of my fellow peregrinos for their assistance in aiding a distressed pilgrim down the mountain.

The day started with the continual climb out of Rabanal Del Camino and my sights set on the legendary and important stop at the Iron Cross. I read last night that at 1515m in altitude, this mountain is the highest point of the entire Camino Frances. Higher than the Pyrenees. Needless to say, today was physically challenging.

It has now been suggested by two people that I leave everything behind up there and to come down the person I want to be. Such a tall order, and one I basically thought about the whole way up. I thought about how wonderful it would be to stand at the base of that famous cross with my offering in hand, say my peace, prayer or mantra and then, ritually, place my coral on the enormous pile of various other offerings

Colleen Davis

and then automatically walk away a new, improved and authentic version of myself. Yes, that would be nice.

The cross itself, was kind of underwhelming, but what it represented was massive. Stone upon stone had been left by the millions of pilgrims that have been there before me. Stones of hope, loss, love and sacrifice. There were pictures of loved ones lost, symbols of gratitude and words of encouragement and love. Like those around me, I wanted to climb to the top, place my coral close to the cross and have my picture taken, and I did, but I felt bad walking on all those other meaningful items that had also once been strategically placed on the mound. I left the coral my grandkids had given me at the top of the pile with a message to "Live your dreams." It was a message not only to them but also as a reminder to myself. I then climbed down and continued to observe others do the same little dance I had just done and then I left. There was no revelation; only gratitude.

I walked with Helene again today. She took my picture at the cross and I hers. Most of the time one of us walked ahead of the other and the conversation was kept to a minimum and that was okay. Just a walk of reflection.

We passed through a few villages, each one relevant to the Way of St. James. One retaining its medieval setting with ruins and tumbled down houses, one settlement that had a population of only nine people and one bearing a monument in tribute to a pilgrim who passed away. It's hard not to notice these things when there are no other visual distractions around. And, it was such a beautiful day to enjoy all these sites and more.

At some point during our very steep descent into Molinaseca, we passed a gentleman who was at a standstill and looked as if he was in a bit of distress. I am not proud to say that when I first passed him, I noticed that his backpack and part of his pants were dirty giving off the impression he had either been resting up against something or he had taken a bit of a tumble. He also looked unsteady on his feet in an area where you really needed to be steady. The moment I passed him with the intent of continuing on, I knew I shouldn't have, so I waited for Helene to catch up to me and suggested we stop and ask him if he needs assistance. By this time, he was slowly making his way towards us, again, looking as if he was going to fall at any moment. During a brief conversation, we learned he was getting very dehydrated and that, earlier on in the day he had taken some medication for pain and was starting to feel a little dizzy. When asked, he did confess that he had already taken a bit of a fall.

Helene and I helped him down to an area off the narrow rocky path and sat him down so he could rest up against a rock. While doing so, we had taken off his backpack and it quickly became apparent that it was way too heavy for the stretch he was attempting to accomplish today. I immediately gave him one of my granola bars and filled his water bottle up with some of my water along with a package of electrolytes I had purchased back home. I specifically kept them in my daypack for this very reason.

I cannot stress enough how important it is to pack the right items in your backpack/daypack and to make sure you know your limit when it comes to the weight you can carry on your back. I totally get the idea of just winging it, going with the flow, being spontaneous and living life in the moment but I am so okay with the amount of research I did on what to have with you at all times. Thankfully, I never did have to use any of the packages of electrolytes I brought for myself, but at least I had them for this situation and it didn't take long to see the positive effect it had on this man. I ended up giving him a few packets so that if this type of thing happened to him again, he would be prepared.

Pilgrims were starting to pass us and, even though a few would stop and ask about the situation, no one was offering any other assistance than a sympathetic look and a few minutes of their time. One French couple stopped and, because this man was also French, spoke to him in their native tongue and translated back to us what was said. They really didn't tell us anything we already didn't know. This man had fallen prior to our arrival, had taken some pain medication earlier in the day and was feeling dizzy and out of sorts. Again, nothing we didn't already know. It just made me sad to think that this man had already fallen once and was still in obvious distress. We could see that, so why couldn't anyone else who had passed him before we did?

It was getting pretty hot and for every minute we stayed there it was only going to get hotter so, at one point, I looked at Helene and told her that if she wanted to carry on, it would be okay but I was going to stay with this man until we reached Molinaseca. She told me she would do the same and, together, we helped him to his feet and insisted that we carry his backpack to make his climb down the mountain just a little bit easier. His backpack was so heavy, at least twenty pounds, and the thought of carrying his bag as well as my own daypack was as painful as actually doing it. I wasn't going to let Helene carry it because she was already carrying her own backpack. I just had a daypack; she was carrying everything she brought to Spain on her back and it just wouldn't be right.

So, the plan was for me to carry the pack and for Helene to assist the man as we slowly worked our way down the mountain and, that's what we did for a brief period of time. Thankfully, a young man by the name of Matt decided to stop instead of just walking on by, like so many had already done. Matt made the choice to ask us if we needed help. After telling him the back story, Matt took the heavy pack from me and put it on so that his own pack was on his back and the older man's pack was on his chest. We then made a train type line where Helene took the lead, Matt behind her, the older man behind him holding on to Matt's shoulders and me taking the rear, ready to catch this guy if he fell. As we gingerly worked our way down the mountain it is important to note that it was extreme. The guidebooks will tell you the descent is "long and very steep" and it was. It was no longer about me or my journey, no more taking in the surroundings and capturing every moment. It was now an exceptionally slow descent with one goal in mind, don't fall and don't let anyone else fall. It was all about putting one foot in front of the other and being very aware of where you actually placed each foot. This unexpected turn of events probably added another two hours to our day, but I was not about to leave this man until we were in Molinaseca.

At one point, Matt started to struggle with the two bags. He was young and pretty fit, but the older man's bag was literally heavier than his own and it was starting to get very uncomfortable for him. Although I had previously offered to take the pack, literally, off Matt's shoulders, this time I insisted on taking it and, for the next forty-five minutes, I wrestled with it myself. It was painfully heavy, painfully uncomfortable and painfully painful. It must have been a combination of adrenaline and the intense focus I had not to fall that allowed me to ignore the pain I was in and make it as far as I did with this backpack strapped to my back.

It wasn't until we had finally made it down the mountain and got to more even ground that Matt took it back.

Feeling a little bit steadier on his feet, the older gentleman who, unfortunately, I don't remember his name, was especially grateful and offered to buy us all a drink once we got to where we were going and we all readily accepted.

We followed the river Meruelo into Molinaseca but not before first taking a glance at what we were walking into. It was amazing. Another gorgeous Roman bridge welcomed us to the village of eight hundred and eighteen inhabitants, a bridge draped over a river that continued on its own journey. We also passed the Sanctuary of Nuestra Señora de la Angustia, whose construction dates back to the 17th century. Making note to revisit that later, I continued on with the rest of the group, crossed over the bridge and found a wonderful place right on the river called the Meson Puente Romano. We sat on their spacious deck, enjoyed our beverages and had a wonderful conversation. The older man called us all "true brothers and sisters of the Camino" before getting into his taxi that would take him to Ponferrada.

After finding my hostel and having a quick shower, I reconnected with Matt and, together, we explored the village. We then sat and had another drink by the bridge. This time I made the effort to dip my toes in the river, which felt amazing after the day we just had. After going our separate ways, I continued to explore the streets of this cute little village and made my way back to the Sanctuary but, unfortunately, it was closed and all I could do was admire the outside view of this beautiful building.

Going back over the day in my mind, I realize that I came down that mountain the person I want to be. Caring and helpful without expectations or strings. I want to have the time and patience to always choose to do the right thing. Too many times I see people thinking only of themselves without any consideration for their fellow person.

The compliment the older gentlemen gave us that day with regards to being the "true brothers and sisters of the Camino" really touched me. It's weird, because I am that person who will stop and lend a hand to a stranger and I am the one who will stop what I am doing to go help a family member with whatever it is they need assistance with. It is something that just comes naturally to me and, at times, I tend to think maybe it has become expected of me from the person or people asking the favors. I don't do it for the accolades, I do it because that is who I am. I have been thanked for my generosity and I have been told how "special" and "caring" I am, but those compliments are always received with embarrassment or deflection with "Don't worry about it," or "Anyone would have done it." But, the weight and sincerity of those words spoken by that older man that day deserved the respect to be heard and accepted as his truth and I was really blown away by them. Maybe it was partly due to the situation we found ourselves in or the sacredness of the path we were walking on or, maybe, it was because I was finally open enough to recognize that I was worthy of this man's compliment. No, not everyone would have done it. That was obvious considering the number of people who walked right past us. Being one of the "true brothers and sisters of the Camino" is a compliment I actually heard, allowed to resonate and one that I will wear proudly. It is one I will never forget.

I also break today down as one huge metaphor. The climb up the mountain, at times, was difficult and hard which I see as representing the struggles of letting go. Even though this is a life I want to leave behind, it is still hard to say goodbye. I'm not saying everything needs to go. There are certainly changes that need to be made and certain aspects of it that need to disappear. But I have to recognize there are particular facets of my life, my beliefs and traits that have been around for a very long time and they have served their purpose. They have provided protection in the best way they knew how and it is time to let them go. As much as the climb today was tough, so is the decision and the action of letting go.

The descent down the mountain represented the unknown. Having to decide which path offers the lesser chance of falling and then trusting I took the right one while never looking back. Taking the smallest of steps while still moving forward and realizing that sometimes a person just can't do it alone. You may not want to ask for help but be willing to accept it when the right person (or people) come along. Today, I was the one lending a hand and that man had to trust that we had his back, literally. Tomorrow, it might be me who needs the help.

Going through this journal I wrote almost three years ago is very therapeutic and very nostalgic. It is also a reminder of all the "stuff" that came up for me along the Way and how much actually got thought about while I was walking, whether it was me talking to myself silently or sharing conversations with others. The Camino, among other things, is really just a very long therapy session. I don't care who you are, if you have walked a Camino or two or three and don't agree with that last sentence, you are lying.

Tonight, is being spent at the Hotel Meson El Palacio, a wonderful little hostel that sits right at the base of the Puente De

Molinaseca. I am lucky enough to have a wonderful view of the Rio Meruelo and equally as lucky to be able to end my day with a video chat with Lukas. Wishing him a "Happy Birthday!" and allowing our visit to, once again, fill my cup, I settle in for the night. I can honestly say that today was an exceptionally good day!

CHAPTER 27
June 15, 2019: Molinaseca to Cacebelos – 24 km

Today, I am grateful for my back for being able to carry the weight of an extra pair of shoes, along with the various other items in my daypack. Because of that, I was able to switch over to my sandals when my toe got too sore to stay in my sneakers. I am grateful for the Camino for being relatively easy today as my entire body is still feeling the effects of yesterday's adventure. I am especially grateful for the sun which is currently shining down on me as I sit on a beautiful patch of grass along the river's edge taking in the gorgeous views that surround me which, once again, includes a beautifully designed bridge.

The walk, today was not only pleasant because of how less demanding it was compared to yesterday; it was also one of those days where the Camino meandered through several small villages with large amounts of character. The morning hike leading out of Molinaseca was done on a sidewalk paralleling the main road. That segment was very well marked and I felt confident enough that even if it wasn't, there was absolutely no way for me to take a wrong turn. This allowed my mind, body and soul to slowly wake themselves up and align with one another. I don't know if any of this makes sense, but it gave me the time to feel things out, to assess how I was feeling mentally and physically without having to worry about getting lost. I was getting all the kinks out in a nice relaxing way.

Soon, the path turned into just that, a path. An earth trail that weaved its way through the rolling hills and vineyards. I'm sure when the fruit trees are ripe for the picking and the vines are overflowing with grapes, the scenery is a bit more breathtaking, but for now the fields are somewhat bare and that, in itself, has its own charm.

I will never get over, and will probably never be able to articulate it in just the right way, how the Camino has the ability to affect every aspect of my being. Each evening I read about the day ahead in order to prepare myself and to make sure I am equipped with things I will need. I had obviously read somewhere in my guidebook that I would be walking through Ponferrada and passing by one of its historical landmarks, but reading about it and actually doing it are two totally different things.

So, there I am, walking through Ponferrada and I am literally saying to myself out loud, "Well, there's a castle!" And, not just a castle. A sprawling fortress with a moat and a drawbridge. And, it's not like that was even the first castle I have come across during this journey, but it's what this castle and every other amazing structure I have stood beside and admired represent. They all just solidify the fact that I am here. I am literally here and I am walking by a castle.

What I was admiring was the Castillo de Los Templarios or Castle of the Templars which is considered the most remarkable castle in Northwestern Spain because it's origins date back to the first Iron Age and welcomed the Knights Templars in 1178.

A lot more sidewalks, streets and pavement led me out of the city and through more towns and villages, all of which just seemed like small suburbs of Ponferrada. Sometimes I would see the name of the village I was about to walk through on a sign prior to entering and, then others, I'd have no idea their names and I wondered if the villagers just preferred it that way. Are we even welcome here or have they just grown so accustomed to people walking through their land that they don't really even see us anymore?

I stopped at one small village and took a picture of a dilapidated building that had once been someone's home and I thought to myself, "How long did this family hold on to this before they were forced to abandon it?" It was one of those things that brought up so many questions I really wanted to know the answers to but knew I never would find them. I not only felt bad for the people who had to walk away from something that, I want to believe, they loved and had provided them with a lifetime of memories, but I found myself feeling bad for the structure as well. I'm sure in its day, this building was really quite charming and maybe even filled with the laughter and the cliché "pitter patter of little feet," but now it just looked withered, sad and dejected.

The closer I got to Cacabelos, the more pleasant the landscape became. The days trek was noticeably less demanding in terms of the ebb and flow of the elevation but I also think my body is starting to acclimate to the terrain. I have noticed that even when there is an upward climb or, in all fairness, when I have to walk downhill as well, it is becoming generally more tolerable to do the farther from Saint-John-Pied-de-Port I get.

Arriving in Cacebelos, I checked into my lodging which is the Hostel Santa Maria, a nice clean place a short distance from the town square and right next to a market. After taking care of some things and cleaning up a bit, I went out and explored and, eventually, found this beautiful spot by the side of the River Cua. Sitting there enjoying the view, I started to feel a bit overwhelmed. Not because of the physical distance I have travelled today but because of the emotional things that are now coming up. It was in this quiet solitude I realized I have only eight more days of walking and that makes me sad and a little bit anxious. This is coming as a bit of a surprise to me considering I have already been walking now for twenty-four days and, maybe, I honestly thought I would be ready for it to be over by this point. But it is very clear that the end is coming and it is coming way sooner than I want it to. I would gladly change my free days in Santiago de Compostela and in Paris just to continue walking. I really don't want this feeling of total peace and freedom to end. Right at this very moment, even as my toe throbs to the same beat as my heart, I am content. I had a terrible night's sleep last night thanks to a dog who wouldn't stop barking, a church bell that wouldn't stop ringing and my legs that wouldn't stop moving and still, right now, I am content and it is painfully obvious that I haven't felt content for a very long time.

I am scared that I won't know how to maintain this feeling and this way of being when I get home. Even though it is imperative and necessary that change is due, I am scared. And, I realize it is pretty easy to sit at the bank of a river in Spain and plan out how things will go when I get home but what I am not factoring in are the actions, reactions and plans of those whose lives will be affected by it all. I can't predict the narrative once I am placed back in the situation I left behind and that is scary. Being here alone, I can see as clear as the sky is now, how important balance needs to be in my life and how necessary it is to place my own well-being above others. I am no good to myself or anyone else if I go back home and fall back into the same version of myself that I was before I left. I want to become the best version of myself, my authentic self.

I ponder what I would like my world to look like when I get home and I think about all the things I need to let go of. Walking the Camino has definitely proven to me that you don't need very much at all to be happy. Do I still want my race car? Yes! I love going to the racetrack and being a part of the racing scene. Do I think I hold on to too many "things" or "items" with the thought that one day they will come in handy or I will, all of a sudden, need them? Yes! But I am realizing I don't need "things" to make me happy. Do I think I can be a pushover and that I allow people to take advantage of my generosity? Yes! Pleasing other people, with no real thought of what I want, is not going to make me happy.

Don't get me wrong, I know I will always have responsibilities and that my family dynamics will always be there. And I am very aware that my reality is back at home. I totally understand that nothing back there is changing. Garry is getting up every morning and going to work. He will come home, make himself something to eat, maybe work out in the shop and then end his evening in front of the TV, eventually fall asleep to some random YouTube video. I get all that. But right now, I am in Europe. I have completed three quarters of a five-hundred-mile hike across Northern Spain and I have done it alone. I jumped in with both feet having absolutely no idea what I was doing or getting myself into and I need to take that courage and strength that got me here and take it back home with me.

Because I used my journal for the body of this book, the wording may not always have that "professional writer" quality but, I have never proclaimed to be a professional writer. What I wrote was raw, real and expressed while in the moment. At times, the emotions were so strong that the pen on paper could barely keep up with the feelings that were coming up and out. I, myself, appreciate and take more stock in that type of narrative over all the "gloss" and "fluff" some others may prefer to include in order to make the story a bit more appealing.

At times I feel somewhat disconnected to the words I know for a fact, I wrote. I get so wrapped up in the story that I forget it was actually me writing it. Other times, I feel disappointed in myself over those same words. Disappointed for being so motivated and ready for change. Vowing to myself that things would be different after I got home and now feeling like not enough change has actually happened. I read back on some of the revelations and "aha" moments I had throughout my pilgrimage, all the amazing conversations I had with myself and others and, it was really starting to sound like I was getting it all together. But now, as I sit here at my work station, I can honestly say that I have fallen back into some of the old routines.

But then I have to take a loving step back and remember a few things. It has been almost three years since I boarded that plane to Europe and since then, I, like everyone else in the world, have been trying to hold on to some form of sanity as we maneuver through this Covid-19 pandemic. I was home for only six months before the world, as we all knew it, very quickly started to come crashing down. At least I had that time to relive my journey with those who wanted to hear about it – in person. I was lucky enough to have been able to come home and go right back to work. (At least for the first nine months as I work in an industry hit extremely hard by Covid). I was given the time to reflect and focus my efforts on those little steps of personal change I had vowed to take before the Vid took over our lives. I feel for those who completed their journey and weren't given the opportunity to sit with their experience before their lives were affected by Covid and my heart aches for those who attempted to go and were sent back home because of the *pandemic. I mean, for most people, the Camino is a once in a lifetime journey, a soul-searching exploration. Not to be confused with a "holiday" but, rather, a therapeutic quest that should not be ignored or placed on hold. The very moment the Camino Frances was brought up in a conversation I knew in my heart that I HAD to do it and I am really not too sure where I would be right now had I been denied that opportunity.*

Because of the pandemic, my child and their partner made the very tough decision to uproot their entire lives in a city they adore and moved back home. No longer feeling safe in a big city, they felt they could "ride it out" in a smaller town. A decision that not only affects their lives, but mine and Garry's as well. We have made it work but, again, this unexpected event has taken front seat to any focus I had on myself. And, because of their decision to move back home, I have learned new things, done new things and have had some great times with them both.

During this time, my grandmother suffered a stroke and was in hospital for five months. While there, she contracted Covid and went into a period of delirium. While in total isolation and lockdown, I was allowed into her room in attempts to bring her back to reality and make her feel safe when she honestly believed she was in danger. Because of the stroke, it became obvious she could no longer live on her own and we, as a family, came together and guided her through the steps of transitioning into assisted living. I took the lead in packing up a two-bedroom apartment, alongside my mom and dad. A task that would have been placed solely on my mom's shoulders and I am glad I was there for all of them.

So, when I look at all that has transpired since my return home or start feeling like a total failure, I just have to remind myself of those things and then tell myself it is okay. I may not have changed my entire world and I may have fallen back into some of the old routines, but I have to believe I am exactly where I need to be right now. Rome wasn't built in a day.

It is currently 3:10 pm and while the rest of the town is having a siesta, I am enjoying a Coke Zero and an apple pastry outside of the Saint James Way Restaurante while watching the world go by. I walked by a large supermarket earlier, which always makes me happy. Again, I have really come to appreciate the joy in all the little things. Finding a supermercado these days means stocking up on supplies, snacks and dinner for this evening, which I already know will be a pre-mixed salad of some kind.

I have arranged for a video chat with Garry this evening at 5:00 pm "Spain time" which will be 8:00 am his time. For some reason, I get the feeling that I either need to ask him something or tell him something and, for the life of me, I can't think of what it is. I know it probably has something to do with our relationship but, at this time, I don't even know if I care to remember what it is. Hearing the answer to whether or not he misses me isn't something I need to hear. Maybe an appreciation for me? And, even as I write this, I realize I'm not really too interested in knowing the answer to that either. Hearing the answer only means I would have to ask the question and that type of thing is better received when it is volunteered by him and not asked of him. I might want to know one day, but today isn't it. Right now, at this very moment, I am more interested in knowing why I can be so content with doing absolutely nothing here, yet at home, I have to be constantly doing something. Random thought? Or is it because I am not trying to avoid anything here? Hmmm, another "aha" moment maybe.

Random quote of the day I found written on a large stone on the Camino: "You can't go back and change the beginning, but you can start where you are and change the ending."

CHAPTER 28
June 16, 2019: Cacabelos to Las Herrerias– 27 km
Happy Father's Day, Frank!

The start of my day was amazing. I was up and out before the sunrise and, besides a small amount of road walking, I was pretty much surrounded by vineyards all the way to Villafranca del Bierzo (which was just over 7 km from where I started).

Set in a valley and enveloped by mountains, Villafranca is home to three huge churches and one massive castle and, yet, I still found it to be charming and "cute". It was in Villafranca in the 16th century where the Pope allowed pilgrims who couldn't make it all the way to Santiago de Compostela because of illness or injury to enter the Church of Santiago and receive the same absolution as those who made it all the way. There are writings about Villafranca from 1120 about it being an important stop on the Camino and here I am calling it "cute". Even though there are times where I feel the historic magnitude of the Camino is lost on me, I never feel like I am missing out. I may not be able to articulate it, but I definitely can appreciate and be overwhelmed by my surroundings.

Because it was so early in the morning when I walked through the village, there was really no other reason to stop than to take advantage of a few photo opportunities. More lasting memories to prove to myself and to anyone else who cares, that I was actually here.

After leaving Villafranca, the Way pretty much stuck to a main road. I want to say "highway" but there were very few vehicles travelling on it. Sometimes, I would be walking on just the hard shoulder and others, a concrete barrier separated me from the road itself. The beautiful scenery reminded me of the Fraser Canyon back home; a similar road tucked away in a valley and surrounded by mountains. That visual beauty could not take away the fact that the rest of the day was literally spent walking on pavement either on some form of a slant or going strictly uphill and there was nothing enjoyable about that. Road walking in my sneakers was proving too much for my throbbing toe so, when I still had about 9 km to go, I slipped out of my sneakers and into my sandals. Having said that, there was an opportunity where I could have taken an alternate route that cut into the mountains instead of along the road, but my guidebook advised that, even though it wouldn't add distance to my day, it would add some climbing. Adding an unnecessary uphill hike on the eve of the most difficult day of the entire trip - no thank you.

What made this day even less enjoyable was the fact I was back in my head. At this point, it shouldn't come as a surprise but, rather, invited. I mean, isn't this the reason I am on this path? What got me there was the video chat I had with Garry last night. At one point in our conversation, he mentioned that going two weeks without seeing or hearing from me was way too long and we needed to keep in touch more often. My response to that was one of admission that I was fine with the long gap in between chats and how I really wasn't missing too much from home. Well, the look on his face instantly made me feel guilty and I have been carrying that guilt around all day. I probably shouldn't have been so matter or fact, but what was the alternative, more video chats? That's not why I am here. He also asked if I was "having fun and meeting a lot of cool people?" A great question to ask someone who is on "holiday" but he knows why I am here and it really irked me when he asked that because he (of ALL people) knows this isn't a vacation. Yes, I am meeting cool people, but he could have come up with a more relevant question.

To me, it seems like he keeps everything at the surface and because of that, he hasn't allowed any of the real meaning behind all of this to sink in. I literally told him the morning before departing to France that we, as a couple, may not survive the journey I was about to undertake. Could there not have been a better, more appropriate question he could have asked me other than "Are you having fun?" This is seriously the hardest thing I have done in my whole life. It is physically, emotionally and spiritually draining and it constantly feels like I am in a never-ending therapy session. It is like going to counselling every day for thirty-two days straight and that while you are in therapy all day, every day, you are also walking on a treadmill the whole time and the counsellor is the one in control of the speed and elevation of that treadmill.

The whole time he was talking last night, my feet were aching, my knees were sore and my toe was throbbing. And, he is well aware of what this is doing to me physically, but he talks about all the things he is doing at home. Working long hours, working on the car, grocery shopping and maintaining the yard. He then joked about how we will have to sell everything because it is all just too much for him. Does he not realize he is describing my everyday life? Does this now mean he will finally appreciate me a little bit more because of this? Probably not.

I am hoping when I get back home, we will be able to discuss how lobsided our chore lists are and attempt to find some kind of balance so that neither one of us feels overwhelmed but, right now, I can't shake the guilt I am feeling for saying what I said to him last night. I guess I will take the advice that was given to me by my Camino Guru, Dee, when he said that guys don't need much to stay in a relationship. They need acknowledgement and appreciation. So, when I get WiFi, I will have my mom send a message to Garry telling him how much I appreciate everything he is doing back home, because I do. It has been easier destressing knowing that he is back home "holding down the fort".

The answer to whether or not he realizes how much I do around the house, for our household, and for him or whether he appreciates and recognizes me for all that I do is "I don't know." Almost three years post Camino, if he does recognize any of that, he has a really weird way of showing or saying it. If I have learned one thing it is that people only change if they want to. If "forced" change is placed upon them, that particular change will be short lived. If I want change, I have to be the change. And, again, I am a work in progress and need to be kind to myself when it comes to any decisions I make or don't make regarding these matters. Our relationship may have stalled, hit a road block or maybe even come to a crashing halt and, at some point, I know and understand this will all need to be re-assessed, but now is not the time. I am not blind to the situation but, does that mean we go our separate ways? Does it mean we remain together but with an understanding that the dynamics of this relationship will change? Do we attempt counselling? I honestly don't know the answer. I have put this on the back burner for many reasons and, for now I am fine with that. I will re-visit it when I feel strong enough to do so.

About 2 km outside of Las Herrerias the scenery started to change. Although still in the Province of Leon, I am told the difference in the landscape is very much Galician. I start to see more farmland with small rectangular buildings on stilts that, even I know, are designed to protect the grain inside the buildings from rodents and moisture.

I arrived in Las Herrerias and my lodging for the evening, Capricho de Josana. An old refurbished stone home that is, conveniently, situated at the entrance to the village. It offers a good-sized room with a bathtub and an outside patio area for dining. After freshening up, I went out exploring, which didn't take very long considering it is a very small village set in the valley with just one road cutting right through it.

During my exploration, I came across a tree by the river. Someone had placed a sign by it that read "What are your Dreams?" Hung on the tree itself were small rolled up pieces of paper where many took the time to scribe their innermost aspirations, hopes and dreams before, not only placing them on a branch, but sending those words out into the universe. Before moving on, I did the same.

I also passed by a few horses that were casually grazing in a field and, while trying to coax them over for some love time, I was reminded that these horses are there to rent for the climb up to O Cebreiro, a climb that, according to everything I have read, is the most challenging climb on the whole Camino Frances.

I took heed to those warnings and headed back to my room for a soak in the tub, but not before detouring to the patio to order some dinner. I made my order and then proceeded to sit for longer than I had intended to. This is becoming common on the Way as more and more faces become familiar. I talked to a German fellow who is walking the Camino with his dog. His stories are interesting but it is his constant jovial demeanor that I admire. I usually see him after the day is done, always with a drink in his hand and a woman by his side. This evening both him and his companion had had "one too many" but they were so entertaining that it made it very hard to leave but, before my sub sandwich got too cold, I said my goodbyes and made my way up to my room.

Today was a hard day both physically and emotionally, but ending it in a nice warm bath while eating the best sub sandwich I have ever had is well worth it. Not only did I have to take a picture of this sandwich because of how amazing it was, I had to call my mom and tell her as well.

Just like how I wrote about the absolutely delicious orange I ate at the start of the Meseta, it's like your body literally has a mind of its own and I am really starting to see that. We may feel we are the ones in control of our bodies, but that is so not true. My body has shown me many times and in many ways that it is the one in control. My body's drive and its will have been put through the ringer by me and my decision to take on this 800 km walk. It screams at me when it needs a break, it pushes me distances that I didn't think I could go and it craves food I normally wouldn't eat at home but that's because it knows in order to get up each day and walk 25-31 kms, I need to nourish it. We, meaning my body and myself, have become more in sync with each other during this journey than we have ever been. That was probably my "aha" moment for the day. Bottom line is – that sub sandwich was awesome!

Today, I am grateful for the bathtub waiting for me at the end of this long hard day, for this beautiful little village I am currently in and I am grateful for Garry for taking care of our "day to day" back home.

CHAPTER 29
June 17, 2019: Las Herrerias to Biduedo – 23 km

When I arrived into Saint-Jean-Pied-de-Port and signed in at the Pilgrim's Office, I was given documentation with helpful information regarding what I was about to embark on. One of those documents was a thirty-four-section illustration on what the daily terrain would look like throughout the Camino and the elevation changes between kilometers. That and my trusty guidebook were both telling me that today was going to be the most challenging. In fact, my guidebook specifically states "This section is by far the greatest challenge of the Camino Frances, regardless of how it is approached." So, I decided to approach it with a positive attitude.

Over 16 of the 23 km were spent going uphill. At times, the terrain was made up of gravel, dirt or shale and then, at other times, it was a mixture of all three. Some inclines were steep, others long and then some were both incredibly steep and very long. The worst of it was probably the climb up to O Cebreiro, hence the horses for rent back in Las Herrerias.

But even before knowing all of this I, once again, woke up ready and prepared for today's climb and I was excited for it. My body was ready, my feet felt good in my shoes and it was a beautiful day for a walk. I told myself to just take it slow and to stop when I needed to stop and rest when I needed to rest. I told myself that this is literally all I have to do today. I have put my mind, spirit and body through so much already and if I thought the Camino was just, all of a sudden, going to become "easy" I'd be a fool. This Camino will literally break you down just to pick you back up again. I have six days left and I want to spend these last days in celebration and excitement for a new beginning.

So, yes, the climb started pretty much as soon as I left Las Herrerias. The day started on pavement but was soon replaced with a path that went through and up the mountain. At one point I actually stopped and said, out loud, "This is exactly what I had hoped it would be." A smile landed on my face and never left. It was almost too beautiful and, in all that beauty, there was no room for complaints. I was so surprised at how well I was doing during this 8.4 km climb and, at times, I was even cheering others on just like some had done for me during my toughest days.

It was during this section that I crossed the border between Lugo and Leon and am now in the Galicia region. With its strong Celtic roots, O Cebreiro is definitely one of the most beautiful villages I have seen along the Way. Situated atop the mountain ridge I had climbed; this quaint little village had a hobbit kind of vibe to it. It is home to unique pre-Roman dwellings called "Pallozas" – round stone huts with peaked straw roofs, hence the hobbit reference.

As I approached the village, I noticed a gift store on my left and immediately walked in. I will take any opportunity to look for my tacky tourist gift and this was definitely one village I wanted a memento of. Having found the perfect item, I went to pay and, after doing so, the gentleman behind the counter handed me a pin. "A gift," he said, as he pointed at the Canadian flag pin I had attached to my daypack. It was designed with the Canadian flag beside a Camino shell flag. I was so taken aback and overjoyed at this kind gesture that all I could get out was a very enthusiastic "Thank you!" Just one more memory of this magical place so that I will never forget it.

While in O Cebreiro, I also visited the Church of Santa Maria Real mainly due to its notoriety for being one of the oldest monuments on the French Road of the Camino de Santiago. It also holds a chalice and paten (bread and wine) that, legend says, became the flesh and blood of Christ. I am not a religious person but I don't think you really need to be to feel moved while in the presence of something that, very well, could be bigger than us all. I couldn't help but feel humbled, in total awe and very respectful of my surroundings.

The path leading out of the village was just spectacular and the views, especially those high above the valley floor, just continued to amaze. After a few more uphill climbs, I reached Alto de San Roque, a place that bore no significance to me until I saw the bronze statue of a pilgrim battling against the wind. I still can't believe it is really the little things that bring so much joy to me on this journey. I had seen this sculpture many times in photographs online while doing my research for this trip. If you google it, you will see picture after picture of peregrinos proudly smiling with this statue in the background and now, here I am, walking the same path they did to get to this place. No wonder they are all smiling in those pictures, they definitely deserve to be. I found it to be a very rewarding and overwhelming moment. And, yes, I had to take a proud and smiley picture of myself with this monument behind me.

Reaching the final summit at Alto de Poio, the day ended with a slight descent into Biduedo, my stop for the night. I was advised that this tiny hamlet would provide me with a unique experience and it most definitely has. Surrounded by four houses and more cows than people; this village is obviously not a huge draw for today's pilgrim; however, I welcomed the peace and tranquility it offered.

The "tiny Hamlet of Biduedo" is how my guidebook described it. I have encountered and spoke with only two people here. The woman at the small restaurant beside my accommodations and another woman who escorted me to my room. I am staying at the Casa Quiroga, a clean and comfortable rural home with a very spacious, but somewhat dark, room. It has a nice rustic common area with a few furnishings to sit and visit with fellow pilgrims; however, there aren't any. I am literally the only one here. For a while I was starting to question if there were, in fact, any locals at all until a farmer drove a herd of cattle right by my window.

It definitely didn't take me long to explore the area. With only four homes and the smallest church on the Camino, my exploration took all of about fifteen minutes. While sitting out on the stone wall earlier writing in my journal and waving to my fellow pilgrims as they walked by, I did see an elderly woman, all crouched over and making her way to the church. Each unsteady and laboured step she took gradually got her across the narrow street until she eventually got to her destination. I know she didn't go inside the church because it was locked (I had tried early). She had some flowers in her hand so I thought maybe her plan was to place them somewhere outside of the building but from the time it took me to look down at my journal and look back up to see where she had crept off to; she was gone. Like a ninja who could barely move not one second prior; she was no more. Like, she had totally vanished. I am pretty certain that she was, in fact, a ghost.

Without the distraction of people, I was able to reflect on what I had accomplished today. This definitely was a momentous day for me and, I can confidently say, for anyone who has walked this section of the Camino Frances. What I got out of today was:

1. Change isn't easy but you have to just keep moving forward; climbing over any obstacles that may get in your way.

2. I have the ability to persevere. My strength and drive really shined today. I am very proud of that.

3. The fight for what you want is so worth the reward you get in the end.

I could go on and on considering the "high" I must be feeling, having accomplished what I did today. I hope all the other people who did this section today or will be doing tomorrow or maybe even the next, feel the same way I am feeling right now.

Tomorrow I will end in Sarria and that is somewhat bittersweet. Sarria not only marks the last 110 km of the Camino Frances but it is also where many people start their adventure. You really only have to walk the last 110 km to get your Compostela in Santiago. Only six more days to go but I am really not ready for this to end.

Three things I am grateful for today are: the Camino, for providing such a stunning backdrop during the hardest part of this journey. My shoes, for forming so well to my feet today knowing (like they knew?) that the struggle would have been way worse had my feet been unhappy. My courage, for bringing me to this day. The courage that scooped me out of a "comfort zone" that really wasn't all that comfortable and brought me here, to a quaint little hamlet in Spain that, from what I can tell, only has four houses, a few chickens, a bunch of cows and, apparently, one ghost. I feel amazing today and it is all thanks to the courage I had to take a leap of faith.

Colleen Davis

CHAPTER 30
June 18, 2019: Biduedo to Sarria - 22 km

     I didn't sleep very well at all last night. My toe was throbbing and my lower back was very sore. I'm pretty sure it is from all the downhill walking I did yesterday. There was more downhill today and still more expected for tomorrow. As for my toe, with only five more walking days left, there's really nothing more I can do than what I've been doing. Elevate and soak when possible.

     In spite of the lack of sleep, I was up and out of Biduedo by 6:30 am. It's pretty hard to concentrate on the aches and pains when you are surrounded by the beauty that only the rising sun can deliver. When the air is still crisp, the silence of the morning is glorious and the morning mist is dancing on the fields before you.

     Passing a few farming villages, I ran into Helene in the little town of Triacastela and we walked the remainder of the day together. Carrying on with conversations we had had during our previous time together, we both admitted that we were concerned we will lose this sense of freedom and the pure magic of the Camino upon our arrivals back home, but then both agreed that we just can't let that happen. For our own health, well-being and happiness, we can't lose what we have gained here.

     Little did either of us know that we would spend the next twenty-four months and counting in a global pandemic. We were amazing at giving those pep talks and it was great to say something and be instantly validated by her acknowledging that she felt the exact same way. I remember she would say something and my mind would instantly be blown because it was like she was telling my story.

I don't talk often with Helene, but we do check in from time to time and, I hope one day our paths will cross again. I can't speak for her, but this pandemic has certainly been a strain on my mental health, happiness and overall wellbeing but, I'm not going to use that as an excuse for reneging on the commitment to not lose sight of what my Camino provided. It's called "life" and no matter what the excuse is that one may want to use, it is hard to stay committed to such major goals when unprecedented barriers start popping up. Sometimes, it just feels so much easier to fall back into the familiar. Easier maybe, but no longer comfortable. Knowing and feeling what I experienced on the Camino just amplifies all the old behaviours and situations when they happen, making it extremely hard to ignore or accept them anymore. But, thanks to this pandemic and the ball it started rolling, I just don't have it in me to make any massive changes right now. Believe me, I have made changes and stayed true to many of my Camino promises, but I am also very aware of where more change is needed and I'll get there.

We also did something today that, I believe, unloaded so much unwanted weight off of both our shoulders. We shared "secrets". I can't even explain what came over me, but it just felt safe and so freeing to share things I have never said out loud before. Walking with someone I just met, in a country that neither one of us are from, no backstory between us – it just felt safe and right. The things she shared with me were in confidence and are not mine to share and I hope she can feel comfort in knowing that they will be kept that way. Some I could definitely relate to and others not so much so all I did was listen and sympathize.

When she was done, I shared a few of my own. Toxic waste that had been outstaying its welcome down in the pit of my stomach for too long. Things that I have never told anyone before today. I feel I have been pretty open about my life, especially with my mom, but there are things that I have done or were done to me that I have kept tightly locked away. I told Helene things about my family and how, knowing the information I know, has changed my perspective on the dynamics. The lies told in my family, on both sides, are ridiculous and unnecessary. The "secrets" that can never be spoken, the truths that will remain hidden until one of us finds the courage to put up their hand and say "Enough is enough!" Maybe it will be me, maybe not.

I shared with her the final lie that broke the camel's back with Garry. He has been telling me stories since the day we met and I honestly don't understand why. But this one was just after his heart attack, so less than four months ago, and it was about something so stupid. The lie itself upset me, but what upset me even more was how easily it came out of his mouth. That day, I took off my wedding ring and told him I no longer wanted to be in a marriage that was based on lies. I told Helene that the marriage I have been in since the car accident is no longer the one I want. I want a marriage based on trust. A marriage with mutual respect, friendship, kindness, laughter, joy, compassion, tenderness and a genuine interest in one another. There is no room for lies, no need for lies. I am so sick of lies.

I told her that I can't, and won't, go back to the life I had. Not with work, Garry or those in my life who are toxic, ones who don't have my back, treat me like shit or take advantage of my kindness. It is imperative that I bring the Camino home with me and she agreed that she has too as well. It just felt so good to speak my truth out loud to someone who, I know, will do absolutely nothing with it. It was so nice to just speak the deceptions that have been eating their way through my body and have the burden of them bounce off Helene's ears and then come to rest on the Camino trail where they will remain, along with so many other stories and truths spoken before me and long after I leave this path. I felt lighter afterward and I hope she felt that way too after sharing the stories she shared with me.

Can I have what I am looking for with Garry? Well, after almost three years since my Camino, I am still asking myself that question. Still hopeful, but I am not going to wait forever to find out. There have been little changes, but no real significant ones. I still haven't put my wedding ring back on. Instead, I wear a ring I purchased on the Camino. It's sad, but I feel more connected to what my Camino ring symbolizes than I do my own wedding ring.

Reading this last paragraph over, I can say I don't feel alone in those words. I feel I wrote what others are thinking and feeling, but just haven't put them on paper and thrown them out into the universe for others to read. It may not necessarily be a wedding ring per se, but I am sure there are those out there who can admit that they feel more connected to the meaning behind something about their Camino than they do to certain things back home. It's the Camino's magic powers. It grabs hold of you and never let's go. Everyone who has walked a Camino has brought something home; a trinket or souvenir of some kind. All you have to do is look at that item and, I bet, what it first symbolized to you is just as strong now as when you first bought it. If you didn't bring home a tangible item then all you have to do is start talking or thinking about your Camino or, maybe, go back and read a journal you kept and BAM, the connection is there and it is strong.

Today, we were given the option of two routes. We could follow a more direct route to Sarria or, if we felt we could handle the distance, we could add an extra 6 km to our day and head up to Samos to visit the oldest and largest monastery in Spain. Unfortunately, because of the pain I woke up in this morning, I didn't feel comfortable adding more pressure to an already battle worn body. Helene also decided that she would take the more direct route with me.

One highlight of today was a rest stop at an eclectic little back yard area that I would never again be able to give directions to because it seemed to just appear out of nowhere. I can only imagine that it was created by someone who, not only supports their fellow pilgrims, but has probably walked the Camino a time or two themselves. The whole area had been transformed into a refuge for pilgrims to stop, eat, drink and rest. There was a covered sitting area lined with a mishmash of couches and chairs to lounge in, an array of food to select from and the décor could only be described as "unique." Of course, donations were appreciated and I had no problem dropping some coins in the basket. Of all the intriguing objects adorning the area, the one that stuck out the most for me was a trestle with shells hanging from it. People were encouraged to hang their Camino shells on this structure, but not before taking one of the available Sharpies and writing on the shell, itself, the one thing you want to leave behind. A symbolic gesture allowing that person the ability to move forward without the weight of what has been holding them back.

I didn't hang my shell, but as I stood there reading from those who had, I saw that they all seemed to be carrying the same type of message. What did people, like myself, want to leave behind? Fear, anger, resentment, their old life. This heavily weighted trestle was telling me that the human race is more alike than different. People from all walks of life and from all over the world, colour, creed, orientation – it just doesn't matter. What remains on this trestle are the burdens left behind, I have no idea who wrote them, what they look like or where they came from. All I know is that they wrote exactly what I would have written and because of that, I don't feel alone.

Choosing to go the direct route to Sarria meant there were very few places to stop at. It was also noted that it would be a bit hillier than the other option, but because I didn't take the alternate route, I really have nothing to compare it to. All I know is that the path I took was filled with the beautiful scenery of rural Galician landscapes. We passed by more horreos; those structures built on stilts. Some made of wood with straw type roofs and others built out of stone. We even had to step clear off the path once to make room for a cattle rancher who was being followed by his large herd of cattle.

We had been walking along a lovely path lined with lush greenery when we came upon the little hamlet of Ramil. There was a clearing in the path just before arriving that opened up to a chunk of land with an abandoned stone building resting on it. I say it was abandoned only because it looked abandoned. It very well could have been lived in. It wasn't the building that first caught my eye, it was the commanding presence of a gnarly old chestnut tree welcoming us to the village that grabbed my attention. Apparently, chestnut trees are common in this region but, certainly not on this scale. This thing was not only huge but it was also over 800 years old.

Arriving in Sarria, the antique capital of Galicia, I found my lodging for the night, Hotel Mar de Plata. Rated in my guidebook as a 2-star hotel, I have come to learn that the rating system is a lot different than the rating system back home. It is a very modern and beautiful hotel with all the amenities I could ever need and more and certainly worth more stars than what it has been given.

For the first time in a while, I actually went down to the hotel's restaurant for the Pilgrim's meal. Sitting and eating at a table alone would normally be something I'd avoid, but, as I sat there at my table for one, I looked around the room and found several others doing the exact same thing. I could have easily invited someone to join me but, I just didn't want to. After a full day shared with someone else, I just felt like ending it alone. Of course, the dinner came with wine and when I say wine, I don't mean a glass. A full carafe of red wine was placed on my table and, as much as I tried to drink enough to give the appearance that I had put some kind of dent in the bottle, I just couldn't do it. So, on my way out, I gave it to a table of four who looked like they would enjoy it a lot more than me. Seriously, it is harder to get a glass of water in Spain than it is to get a bottle of wine.

My guidebook advised to take advantage of the amenities the city of Sarria has to offer. To buy some snacks, obtain some money, if needed, and to stock up on any other items prior to continuing tomorrow because there won't be many services available until arriving in Portomarin. Considering Portomarin is another 21 km away, after dinner, I did walk around a bit collecting the items I think I might need. I also did a little sight-seeing. Just enough to get a picture of myself behind the typical touristy structure of the name of the city and some old buildings, but there really wasn't anything in Sarria that I HAD to see so, I retired early and am now up in my room doing all the things I need to do to prepare for tomorrow's hike.

What am I grateful for today? Helene - I am grateful for the day we shared together. I am grateful for that bohemian little oasis we stopped at today and the courage it took those people to write their vulnerabilities on their shells and hang them on the trestle. I am grateful that, even though my toe and back hurt, I am still able to, and want to, walk. Here is to the last 110 km of my Camino!

Today, January 8, 2022, I ordered my credentials from the Canadian Company of Pilgrims website. Why did I decide to share this information? Because, one thing I have learned and am trying to implement in my life is that you have to live as if what you really want is already so. Do I know when I am going? No. Do I know which one I am doing"? Again, No. I have the guidebook for the Camino Portugues but, maybe I will change my mind and decide to do the Camino Madrid or maybe even walk the Camino Frances again. I also ordered some hiking socks. The five finger toe socks that I highly recommend to help reduce the chance of getting blisters. I have a box under my bed that holds items I have started collecting for my next Camino. I have no flights booked, no hotels arranged, nothing other than the desire to go and the mindset that I am going to walk another Camino this year.

CHAPTER 31
June 19, 2019: Sarria to Portomarin - 22 km

Today was a rough one for me physically. I must have really overdone it yesterday because I really felt sluggish today. Almost immediately leaving Sarria, I was faced with a pretty decent 5 km climb followed by a continued and gradual incline that stuck around for most of the day.

What distracts me from the constant climb is the setting I am in. It's walking through rural countrysides and fields of flowers. It's passing by small villages instead of attempting to maneuver through large cities. The Galicia region is beyond beautiful. A lot of moss-covered trees and stone walls, vast farmlands, old oak trees and narrow dirt paths well-worn from all the pilgrims who have travelled on them. There are very few people though. I walk through these villages wondering where all the residents are. The setting, once again, reminds me of the movie Lord of the Rings. Like I am waiting for an army of knights to come galloping down the trail on their trusted steeds, both man and beast in full armor or maybe a displaced peasant family meekly cross my path attempting to sell me their wares. Yup, that definitely describes the environment today. Just natures raw and primitive beauty around every turn.

Somewhere between the villages of Brea and Ferreiros sits the marker stating that Santiago de Compostela is exactly 100 km away. I stopped to take a picture of this very surreal moment and reflected on the fact that the second I left that spot, the remaining kilometers would change from triple digits to double.

I remember when I first started and the sign posted in Roncesvalles read "790 km to Santiago de Compostela" and how scared and overwhelmed I felt. Then, when I reached the halfway mark somewhere near Sahagun and how accomplished I felt and how excited I was knowing I still had half the journey left to go. Now, as I sit here today realizing I have less than 100 kms to go, I am sad that this is ending. What is just as despairing is the shape others have left that marker in. It was so defaced with random words, people's names and other useless scribble that the meaning behind the marker is lost in graffiti. I can totally appreciate the words of encouragement and wisdom strategically placed along the Camino Frances but I don't find any appreciation for what has been done to this marker.

After Ferreiros, the terrain continued to ebb and flow until I got about 7 km out of Portomarin and then it became a solid downhill slope that included a 300 m steep descent from hell. My knees, legs and feet were all working hard today and they were feeling every bit of those transitions.

Reaching the banks of the Rio Mino, I crossed another beautiful bridge that reached out to the entrance of Portomarin. What I found funny was that my guidebook described being welcomed into Portomarin in this way - "across the bridge, up a majestic flight of steps crowned with an arch." Yes, across the bridge was a flight of stairs with an arch at the top but what the guidebook failed to mention was that, after the landscape I had to conquer today, being met at the end of it by the most vertical set of stairs I have ever seen in my life was not welcoming or majestic. I stood at the bottom of that long set of stairs for quite some time trying to talk myself into taking that first step up. It was like the Camino purposely placed those steps there as either a cruel joke or a massive test of my will. Well, I did step up and up and up until

I finally made it to the top where, yes, I was greeted by the beautiful city of Portomarin.

Portomarin kind of reminded me of a little town in Arizona I had visited once called Jerome. A historic copper mining town located near the top of Cleopatra Hill. The town itself has more of an old mining camp vibe to it, but what I found similar is that both places are structurally layered on a hill, meaning, you are always either walking uphill or downhill.

Unlike Jerome, where the town slowly slid down the mountain, Portomarin was once on the opposite side of the bridge until part of it sank into the waters of the Mino in the 1960s. Because of that, most of the significant and historic buildings were moved, brick by brick, up to the top of the hill on the opposite side of the river.

After climbing the stairs that I, not so lovingly, nicknamed "Mt. Everest Jr.," I found my lodging for the night. The Pension Portomino. Like some of the other places I have stayed at, The Pension Portomino's hostel can fit forty people and their separate hotel, located right across from it, has twenty-four private rooms. I am staying in the hotel, which is really nice and big and deserves a higher rating than the 1-star it has been given in my guidebook. As the manager was taking me to my room, I noticed a little alcove attached to the hotel with an outside laundry area, so, after having a shower, I went down and washed all the clothes that desperately needed to be washed. That machine was full.

Once all my laundry was done, I went out to explore the city and then ended up grabbing a table at a local café and sipped on a café con leche. Sometimes, I just like to sit and people watch and what I saw today was kind of sad. At a table next to me were, what I could only assume, a father and son. It's always nice to see families spending time together except for the fact that both of them were on their cell phones. I looked around a little more and saw a husband and wife sitting at another table, both on their phones as well. None of these people were actually talking to each other and that got me thinking. Not once in the last twenty-eight days has a conversation I have been a part of been interrupted by a ringing cell phone. And, not once in the last twenty-eight days have I shared a meal with someone who has had their head buried in their phone. These are moments and memories that these people may never have again and there will come a time when one of those four people won't be around anymore to actually spend this time with. It was just kind of sad to think that these people, at that specific time, couldn't come up with something to talk about with each other.

After making those observations, I ran into Helene who told me there was going to be a special pilgrim's concert at 6:00 pm that she was planning to attend. She had invited a fellow Swede by the name of Gōran, who I had previously been introduced to, and was now inviting me.

I remember seeing Gōran in Hospital de Orbigo. I had finished walking for the day and was enjoying a Coke Zero at a café when I noticed this man sit down at an empty table about two down from me. I was immediately struck by the way he conducted himself, his mannerisms and the way he spoke to the waiter who came out to ask him for his order. The waiter had taken Gōran's order but then proceeded to upsell him on some other items. Gōran said he wasn't interested but the man persisted. Gōran finally looked at the man and said, "All I want is the beer, but if I decide I want something else, I will tell you." He didn't say it rudely at all; he was direct, forward and definitely got his point across. What struck me was the way the statement was delivered with a definite air of confidence that I wished I could pull off and I just got the impression that this was a man who really knew who he was, if that makes any sense. I was intrigued enough to remember him when Helene finally introduced us and I shared that initial observation with him. He just laughed it off.

After heading back to my hotel to get into some "concert" clothes, I met up with Helene and Gōran and we, along with so many familiar faces, entered the Church of San Xoan for this one-man concert. This Romanesque temple, designed to be both a church and a castle, was the perfect setting for such a wonderful performance. The man started off by playing a couple of songs on his flute and then went into Gregorian chanting. It was absolutely amazing and hypnotic. There really isn't any way for me to describe that style and sound of song and still give it the justice it so rightfully deserves. Not once during his performance did he need the assistance of a microphone. The acoustics in this church were perfect.

As I sat there enjoying the music, I intentionally reminded myself to take a deep breath and really soak in this moment because once it is over, I won't experience it again. In this moment and at this time, this is where I am. I also took some time to look around the room and concentrate on the faces of my fellow pilgrims. I wondered what their minds were telling them. I would make eye contact with a few and we would simply smile. I may not know their names or have seen their faces before but, here we are, being a part of each other's moments, experiences and memories. It was such a magical time. At the end of the concert, I was invited to join a group for dinner, but I graciously declined. I was just way too tired and in desperate need of resting my feet.

I just finished my nightly chat with my mom and something she asked has me thinking. "Have you had any more enlightening moments?" Today, I really didn't. It's more of an understanding or a knowing of what has to happen. I need to incorporate everything I have been shown on this Camino into my daily life. I cannot forget how this has impacted my spirit and my soul. I have felt emotions I haven't felt in a very long time. The anger, resentment and stress has been replaced with joy, happiness, self-pride and love and I want more of that. This has been an amazing journey that needs to stay in my life forever. This can be my life.

If only I could have harnessed that moment. Please harness those moments!

When it comes to the mistakes or bad judgements I have made in my life, my mom always says I am "a slow learner" or that I always have to "learn the hard way" and, if I were to actually dive into all those times in my life, it could probably get pretty depressing. I don't like to judge myself for making the same mistakes over again. Believe me, I have people close to me who are more than willing to remind me of those times. But when I feel I may be heading on a path that I have been done before, I can have that stern conversation with myself and ask myself the tough questions, especially, when I read back over how happy I was and how enlightened I sounded on this particular day. I can ask myself, "What are you doing?" "How is this serving you?" and "Is this what you really want?"

I seriously wrote those words in my journal — "This can be my life." Yes, Colleen, it can be, but what are you willing to do to obtain that kind of life?" Well, first off, because I am such a slow learner, I could take another long walk. Already in the works! Secondly, I can really start to dive into what has gotten me back into the position where I feel like another walk is needed. That is something I've been doing more seriously in the last few months and, thirdly, I can do something about it. That one is a bit tougher. I am not saying that I haven't taken baby steps towards doing something about it, but this is the one I have the hardest time with because I care more about how my actions will affect others more than how it will help me.

The anger, resentment and stress have, once again, crept in and, at times, overshadow the joy and happiness and that's not right. Balance — that's all I am after. Just a little bit of balance. I have got to start thinking of myself first, which to most is just a given, but I very rarely think of myself first and that is what's making this so hard. What I consider progress is the fact that I can acknowledge and recognize this in myself and that I am currently working towards eliminating some of the things in my life that are causing me the most stress and anxiety. I now understand and can see what is causing the anger and resentment and I am starting to verbalize this to the people who need to hear it. All in good time.

The three things I am grateful for today are: Frank's knife that I am currently using to cut my cheesecake. I am grateful for my accepting nature (Explained — I have met, talked with and walked beside so many beautifully weird, wonderful and unique people and have felt no judgements towards them regarding the things I have seen and heard.

We are all in this together, working this out together and there really is no room for hate). I am also grateful for the beautiful music at the concert tonight. I sat there, in the moment, and honestly enjoyed something I really didn't think I would.

CHAPTER 32
June 20, 2019: Portomarin to Palas De Rei - 24 km

Today was a great day! There are definitely a lot more people walking the last 110 km. It really starts to become noticeable at the end of the day when I have reached my village/town/pueblo/city. I am usually up and out now by 6:30 am and, even with the addition of more pilgrims, it's not affecting any aspect of my journey. There are no large crowds or long lineups at cafés or anything. It is just becoming apparent that yes, in fact, a lot more people seem to be "around."

I walked alone for most of the morning which seemed to have more of a constant uphill vibe to it than a "see-saw" kind of motion as described in my guidebook. Tomorrow is supposed to be more of the same, just longer. It's like the first part of the Camino tested me physically, the second tested me emotionally and mentally and, although this last stretch is supposed to be about the spiritual journey, it's like the Camino, itself, is just testing my spirit. Almost like it is intentionally stripping me bare one layer at a time. Twenty-nine days of walking and it is still testing my will and desire and by the time I walk into Santiago de Compostela, I will just be one big pile of mush and I won't have any strength left to give to my old life or my old way of thinking. After twenty-nine days of walking, I still find it a struggle, both physically and mentally, to hike up these hills. When will I finally have my spiritual awakening? Or maybe the question should be, "Will I have a spiritual awakening?"

The mornings walk out of Portomarin was really quite stunning. I left while the street lights were still illuminating the path, with the help of the waking sun. There was a little bit of a mist on the river, the birds were chirping and the panoramic views, as I walked back down the hill, were absolutely gorgeous. Most of the day was spent walking among the eucalyptuses on a dirt path that allowed the crunch underfoot to become mesmerizing. Even when I was walking alongside the road, it really wasn't all that bad because the trail was set back from a bit and I felt safe. To top things off, the Galacian architecture has been completely stunning.

I have seriously done more therapeutic talking and thinking in the last twenty-nine days than I have my entire life and today was no different. I may have walked the morning alone, but I was eventually joined by Helene and Gōran and we walked the remainder of the day together. Among many other topics, we discussed how stressful my life is and how extremely important it is for me to rid myself of the various stressors that are damaging my very being.

It wasn't all about me. There was a lot of advice, sympathy and compassion shared as we bouncing things off of each other and it was just so nice to feel safe enough to speak my truth and receive nothing but kindness back. There was no judgment.

Throughout this pandemic, I have tried my best not to judge people. Covid has definitely divided our city, our country, our world and instead of joining in on all the hate, I have stayed pretty much neutral. Not complacent, neutral. I have my own thoughts and beliefs but I am choosing, for the most part, to keep those to myself. I listen to both sides and allow others to share how they are feeling and coping without judgement. Or, at least I am trying not to be judgmental. For those who have chosen to alienate themselves from me or my home because of how we are riding out the pandemic, I won't judge you; things will just be a little different when it is finally over.

Having said that, I need to start being less judgmental of myself. I had a lot of epiphanies, revelations and expectations of myself after my Camino. I came home with the idea that I was going to let go of all the stressors in my life and I didn't. As I sit here and write this, I am feeling more stressed out than ever before. As a matter of fact, two nights ago I had one of the biggest panic attacks I have had in a very long time. I am extremely stressed out about my work, my health, the pandemic and the division it has created and I am stressed about my relationship with my husband. We both currently have family members in hospital, my mom is suffering with a broken rib and not just a half an hour ago my husband fell on some ice and injured his knee. I am awaiting shoulder surgery after enduring my third (and last) cortisone shot and even though I had treatment on my lower back, I have been suffering with constant nerve pain for the last two weeks that no form of treatment seems to be able to ease. I haven't had a good night's sleep in who knows how long and my eating habits have totally gone to shit. But what I seem to be fighting with the most is the self judgement.

I remember that day with Helene and Gōran and I can still hear their words of genuine concern and I let those words soak in and resonate. I probably even convinced myself, once again, that change was definitely going to happen the second I got back home. So, why do I feel like I am right back where I never wanted to see myself again?

I told myself that when including this part of my story (the part in italics) I was going to let it be organic and allow the words to just flow from my brain, to my fingers and then onto these pages and that is exactly what I just did. Today is just that kind of day. So, I am going to sit in this crap without judgement because I am aware of the work I have already done, the steps towards change I have already made and I know that these feelings and thoughts will pass and I will be okay.

The afternoon wasn't all serious. I find that when I am with Helene and Gōran, my laughter comes back. I am genuinely happier when I am in their presence. We took our time on the path and when one wanted to stop, we all stopped and it wasn't out of obligation, it was because we were enjoying each other's company. At one point, Helene looked over at Gōran and said something to him in Swedish. Realizing that I had no idea what she had just said, she translated that what she had just said was, "Isn't she lovely." In that very moment, I realized that the person I want to be, who I used to be, was starting to shine through. And I voiced that. I literally said, "This is the way I used to be. The old Colleen is coming back!" Gōran chimed in and said, "We like this one." You know what, I do too.

I don't remember the specific area we were in, but we stopped and took a break at this little café that seemed to come out of nowhere and was, seriously, placed in the middle of nowhere as well. One minute we are walking amongst the eucalyptus trees or on, what seemed like, an abandoned road and, all of a sudden, there's a little café with tables and chairs out front. I enjoyed a refreshing beverage while Helene and Gōran had a bite to eat.

Just like back at home, I am a very light eater, not much of a breakfast person and can't really eat a lot of things because of stomach issues, so when I walk through a village first thing in the morning, that's exactly what I do, walk right on through. If I am walking with someone who wants to stop and eat, I will either keep going or stop with them but only have a drink or a piece of fruit, maybe one of the pastries I have stuffed in my daypack. Unlike a lot of people here, I don't make a point of finding a nice restaurant at the end of the day or go out of my way to try all the delicacies you can only get here in Spain. I go to the local supermercado and pick up a pre-made salad, cheese and meat snack pack or some kind of sandwich.

My guidebook highlights certain places worth stopping at for a great dining experience or makes suggestions on the perfect town to stop for a break, but I find it really depends on the kind of day I am having as to whether or not I want to take the advice of my book. Some of these villages take about ten seconds to walk through and, because they seem to melt into the rest of the amazing, historic and ancient scenery, sometimes I've passed through three villages before I even think about stopping. But this little café that seemed to just pop up out of nowhere was one stop I welcomed. Again, the trek had felt like a constant uphill battle and my legs and feet needed a bit of a break.

From the moment we left that café, the climb not only continued, but felt like it was just going to go on forever. What really stands out for me was the way the three of us approached it; head down and one foot in front of the other. Gōran was a beast and just kept the same pace the whole way up, but sometimes I would fall back leaving Gōran and Helene to walk together and then sometimes Helene would fall back, allowing Gōran and me a moment together. At one point we were single file and marching up alone, again, heads down and one foot in front of the other. But, at the end of the day, we all strolled into Palas de Rei together.

Because the Camino is starting to get busier, Gōran and Helene are, at times, finding themselves in that whole "bed race" situation.

Where the minute you get to your destination, you immediately head to the nearest Municipal albergue or hostel and, if you arrive too early, you place your backpack in a line outside its doors and then watch the clock at a nearby café or park and wait for it to open. This was the case today so, we parted ways and I went to go settle in at the Albergue San Marcos.

The Albergue San Marcos is beautiful and beautifully located. The second I walked into my room I wanted to immediately run back out to find my two new friends and invite them to stay with me. My room has two twin beds joined together to make one king and beside that is a bunk bed with double sized mattresses. I continue to shake my head at the quality of accommodations I have been so blessed to be staying in. The room is huge and has more than enough amenities to make my overnight stay a comfortable one. The whole back wall where the head of my bed sits up against has been dedicated to hold a mural of the wheatfields I walked through in the Meseta, the room is extremely clean and the hotel itself is very modern.

After freshening up, I went to explore my surroundings and found Gōran sitting alone out front of a café, so I happily joined him. After enjoying a beverage, we went for a walk and met up with Helene and Mary, a fellow solo walker. During our sightseeing jaunt around town, I told Helene and Gōran about the number of beds I had in my room and I let them know that if they were ever stuck for a place to sleep, they were more than welcome to stay with me for the remainder of the Camino. We then went back to my albergue for dinner and enjoyed some more laughs, good food and even better company.

One of the things we talked about during our meal is the idea of walking into Santiago together. I started this journey alone and I fully intended to end it alone as well. Not out of spite, but because the idea of sharing that milestone with other people just wasn't part of the equation. I wasn't expecting to meet up with anyone long enough to want to share that moment with. In the beginning I felt that when that day came, it would be a very private and personal moment – done alone. But now, I don't feel the need to be alone anymore. I don't want to feel alone anymore. I have shared my personal story with these people so why not begin the next chapter of it with them. Even though we didn't walk the whole Camino together, we did accomplish this together. We walked the same path, climbed the same mountains and overcame the same obstacles so this just makes sense. So, if it is meant to be – it will be. If, on that day, we find each other together, we will rejoice in each other's accomplishments as the three Camino Amigos.

The three things I am grateful for today: I am grateful for being open to the idea of sharing a vulnerable yet monumental moment with my newfound friends. I am grateful for having those friends remind me of how lovely I am and I am especially grateful for my newfound friends.

CHAPTER 33
June 21, 2019: Palas De Rei to Arzua - 29 km

I woke up this morning feeling great!

Taking advantage of the free WiFi that 99% of my accommodations have had, I jumped online and saw I had an amazing message from my brother. In it, he mentioned how he was following my progress on Facebook and that he was telling everyone how proud he was of me. Underneath his original post, other people had written words of encouragement that just put an extra spring in my step.

Today was filled with rises and falls as the terrain continues to kick my butt. Warned in advance that this was going to be a strenuous day with lots of hills to climb, I prepared myself both mentally and physically before my early departure. I have grown accustom to doing my shin splint exercises every morning and every night despite the fact that, even though they are designed to help with shin splints, most of them are excruciatingly painful on my big toe. Small concessions can be made to help avoid that particular area but then there are some where, no matter how hard I try, my big toe feels every bit of it.

Departing at my normal time, I was surprised to see how few people were on the trail. It was as if everyone, besides me, decided to sleep in. Once again, the early morning walk out of the city was beautiful and, even though I stopped to admire my surroundings and take a few pictures of things that really stuck out for me, some things just can't be captured in photos. I will always have them as memories but they don't capture the feelings associated with being in the moment. Everything is crisp and quiet; innocent and untouched. It really is hard to explain. I also took advantage of knowing I was alone to turn my phone's video feature on and, while hiking through the eucalyptus forest, sang "Happy Birthday" to my niece, Alisha. It may still be yesterday back in Canada but it is technically her birthday here in Spain and it will be a nice little message waiting for her when she wakes up this morning.

The first 12 km were done without a proper break which, I know, isn't always that smart, but I was just feeling so rejuvenated and good that I just kept going. I did sit for a brief moment in what is known as the best-preserved medieval village along the entire Camino. I sat across from a 13th century church to enjoy some water, have a moment off my feet and just pause to soak in my surroundings. This is all starting to go by so fast that I just want to capture as much of it as my whole being can take in. In moments like these, I just wish I could freeze time. I find that I no longer have to remind myself to soak it all in or appreciate where I am at, it has just now become a part of me. The sights and sounds of the Camino literally surround me from morning to night and I am in a constant state of awe.

A little further down the road, I stopped in the small village of Furelos for a café con leche. I was told by a fellow pilgrim that Gōran and Helene weren't too far behind me so I sat and waited for them to arrive with the hope we could all continue the day together. Furelos has one of the most historical, longest and most well-preserved medieval bridges along this route. It was absolutely stunning. Everything about it just oozed "ancient" and, yet, it will stand long after I am gone. The architecture of these masterpieces is really spectacular. A strong and powerful piece of history that commands attention and admiration and then I just walk all over it. It's really very mind blowing.

My two friends did make it to the café and we continued on together and, almost immediately after departing, we were faced with a good 2 km climb followed by even more long sharp ascents spread out throughout the rest of the day. I may not have taken very many stops this morning but we definitely made several of them during the second half. Whether it was for food and drink, to use a bathroom, change our shoes or just because we all needed a rest, again, when one wanted to stop, we all stopped and it was no big deal. What else did we have to do today other than walk. The path took us through eucalyptus forests and across farmlands, past remains of old stone houses which were now all but rubble and by eclectic and vintage cars randomly placed for our enjoyment. Sometimes the path was nothing more than a eucalyptus leaf covered dirt trail that would slowly blend into an uneven and well-worn brick road until, eventually, the entrance to a town welcomed you with pavement.

I hit the, proverbial, wall in Ribadiso da Baixo, a beautiful little settlement situated right along the river. I only know the name because I thought I had finally reached Arzua and, after passing several pilgrims soaking their feet in the river, was ready to do the same. The albergue they were all at is, apparently, well known for being one of the best along the Camino and, having only seen its outside setting, I can understand why. It looked beautiful. It has also been taking in pilgrims for almost five hundred years. I remembered reading about this in my guidebook and now, having actually passed it, I knew I still had 3 km to go before my day was done and it was all uphill from there.

It took me nine and a half hours to accomplish this stretch today and my body feels it. My accommodation for the night is at the Hostal Residencia Teodora which is located right on the Camino. Rated as a 2-star hotel, it is comfortable and has everything I need. After checking in, having a well needed shower and talking to mom (basically my daily routine) I met up with Helene and we walked around exploring the sights. Gōran then messaged me and we all got together for a drink. With only two more days to go, it has been decided that we will definitely be walking into Santiago together. It just feels right. The three of us have quickly and very easily become this close Camino family. There are many people I have passed or have been passed by in the last couple of days who, even though I haven't been introduced to them, I feel this sense of pride for and I hope to see them walk into Santiago De Compostela where I can share, even from a distance, in their accomplishment and success. We have all put our mind, body and soul through so much this last month that it would be impossible not to be happy for all the strangers who we know so well.

What warms my heart is that both Gōran and Helene are on their own schedule, meaning they really don't have one. Because they haven't pre-booked any rooms or had luggage transferred ahead, they can walk for as long they want each day and stop wherever they want. But they are choosing to stop when I do in order for all of us to be together. I can't speak for them but whenever I stop to accommodate one of their needs, it is done because I genuinely want to be with them. It isn't out of obligation or guilt. It is because I am really enjoying their company. I can only hope they feel the same way.

As I sit here tonight and write in my journal, I am physically, spiritually and emotionally tired. It is time for the talking to stop and the "doing" to start. No more talking or wishing or hoping – it's time to start living the life I truly want. The life that will make me happy.

The three things I am grateful for today are: Ken's message to me first thing this morning and knowing that he is proud of me. That message truly got me where I needed to go today. I'm grateful for my toe nail for hanging in there another day. It just wouldn't be fair to have it fall off now, when we are so close. Hang on little buddy. And, I am especially grateful for my laughter, the one I lost a long time ago. It is great to hear my genuine laugh again.

CHAPTER 34
June 22, 2019: Arzua to Pedrueza - 21 km

I was up and out by 6:30 am to start a day that had more emotional ups and downs than the terrain. Not saying that the ground doesn't still hold all the power in my quest to Santiago de Compostela, I just wasn't noticing it as much as I was noticing what was going on with my body.

My mind was on a conversation I was planning on having with Garry tonight. Even though the message I wanted to send flowed nicely in my mind, I was more concerned about how I would articulate it to him. I just wish he could read my mind but, then again, if he could then maybe I wouldn't be here right now; there wouldn't be a need for it. Even while writing this, I know that I would have missed the "Way" even if I had never heard of it before. It would forever be that longing or "something I can't explain" feeling deep inside me.

I guess you could say that the day was leisurely. 21 km seems short in comparison to some of the longer stretches I have done. I did the first 11 km without a break. This was just one of those days where it just didn't seem necessary. I mean, I would stop and drink some water, I just wouldn't make a picnic out of it where the food comes out and the shoes come off. The first 11 km really didn't offer too many places to stop and rest anyway.

It's hard to describe the scenery to someone who has never experienced unfiltered nature in all of its glory. Surrounded by the vast array of eucalyptus trees, moss and the tranquility that ties them together, I found myself bewilderedly asking how I even got here; how did I ever get so lucky or deserving of this. And then I'd wonder how many other people have walked in the same footprints that I was now walking in asking themselves those same questions. One cannot help but be in awe of what Mother Nature is providing at this moment.

The path, at times, was nothing more than a narrow earth track with eucalyptus trees on one side and a stone wall on the other. The trees made a protective canopy over my head as the ground caught their long narrow leaves that fell from the sky. The moss was taking up residency on the wall itself and everything, from the largest tree to the smallest pebble captured my attention. When you really think about it, I'm pretty much describing a potential horror movie in the making, but it was magnificent. The area demanded the respect I was giving it without any effort at all; it has been standing strong for centuries and will continue to stand long after I am gone. I have never used the word so much in my life but, I am truly blessed.

At some point, I can't remember where, I joined up with Helene and the conversation continued where it had left off, wherever that was. We passed more interesting sights including a restaurant adorned with beer bottles. Over fifty thousand beer bottles. Some with signatures and others with wishes or messages for people, like myself, to stop and read. Then, there were the pallets and wooden shelves that held several tattered and worn-out hiking boots and sneakers that, I could only assume, had been abandoned by their owners. But, instead of throwing them out after almost accomplishing their goal, someone had given them new life and a new purpose by turning them into flower pots. Of all the things I had seen today and of all the little messages I had read, the one that stood out for me the most was a little something someone had written in red felt on one of the many Camino markers that line the Way. It said: "Where are you? I don't know but I am never lost!" I have seen a lot of messages along the Way but there have only been a few that I have actually stopped and took a picture of and this was one of them. A reminder that even though I have no idea where I am going in life and, even though I sometimes do feel very lost, I never truly am. I am exactly where I need to be, even if I have no idea where it is. I just have to trust the process.

Having said that, Helene and I actually did get a little lost today. Maybe not so much lost but rather off course for a bit. My guidebook mentioned that just before coming into Pedrouzo, there would be an intersection with signs pointing in the direction of Arco instead of Pedrouzo. It also said that it may seem a bit confusing but they are, in fact, the same place. That wasn't even the part that confused me. The part that confused me was the instructions that IF I wanted to stop for a drink or food then I should take a left at the intersection BUT if I wanted to just head to town, I should go straight over the road and through the forest. So, Helene and I walked straight over the road but the only entrance back into the forest was a little to the right, so we went a little to the right.

I think we both knew right from the beginning that we had taken a wrong turn but neither one of us was saying anything. We found ourselves in a beautiful and spacious eucalyptus forest and, what made it even more spacious was the fact that we were the only two in it. Yes, we would lightly joke about the possibility that we were heading in the wrong direction but, the funny thing was, we weren't stopping and turning back around. We had more people coming straight at us than passing us and, now that I think about it, maybe they had taken the wrong turn as well but made no attempt to help us correct our possible error. We were pretty committed to this adventure but it was becoming very apparent we had made a mistake in our directions. We finally said enough is enough and turned back around. Turns out we were a mere ten minutes from my pension had we gone left at the sign instead of right. And, we probably added an extra 3 km to the day.

After settling in at the Pension Residencia Maribel, a very bright, clean and beautifully located guest house situated on a very quiet street, I met up with Gōran and Helene and we went for something to eat. A hamburger patty with a fried egg on top with a side of lettuce and tomato. It was amazing.

Pedrouzo is a small village that has been shaped around the Camino and, because it is the last stop before reaching Santiago de Compostela, it offers a lot of services and places to stay for us walkers. That's just a given considering its placement on the Camino. What wasn't expected was the village fair we happened upon. We were just taking an after dinner walk when we stumbled upon it, so we ventured over to join in. Unfortunately, because it was still too early, things were just in the process of being set up. There were a few concession stands, a couple of rides and two large stages being erected. But, because I had that video chat with Garry, I made arrangements with Helene and Gōran to meet up in the morning, said my goodbyes and headed back to my room.

Either Garry was reading my mind all day or my mom had a talk with him before he got on the chat because he was saying all the things I wanted to hear. He was talking about how much he misses me; how much he appreciates everything I do and how much he wants to help out more at home. He said he considers me his best friend and that he wants to start doing more things together. Talk more, go for drives together and make more time to enjoy each other's company. He was literally saying everything that I had just told Helene I needed more of in my life. It was actually really weird. But, the "new me" is going to trust that this is something he actually plans on doing. I am going to give him the benefit of the doubt and believe what he is saying. During our conversation, I decided I would start the process of trusting him by telling him something I hadn't told him before. Information I had previously not trusted him with because when it came to this particular topic, he had proven himself untrustworthy. But tonight, I decided to let that go and give him another chance. I need to take this journey seriously and I need to start "being" the change. It may sound corny, but it is true.

I refuse to go back to the way it was before I left. I used to feel like Garry was my best friend. He used to be my best friend. I remember those days; I crave and long for those days. I don't feel that way today nor will I feel that way tomorrow. In a week, a month or a year? I don't know. I am hoping that with time and a lot of effort, we can get back to being each other's best friend. Only time and hard work will tell.

Lots of emotions are coming up tonight, not only because of the chat I had with Garry but because tomorrow will be my last day on the Camino. It doesn't seem real other than the fact that it is. After I enter Santiago de Compostela tomorrow that will be it. That is where this part of my journey will end. I had one goal each and every morning this last month and that was to get up, get dressed and start walking. Although there were many days where that seemed like a pretty tough goal to achieve, that is literally all I had to do. Eat, sleep, walk, repeat. Sometimes it was the terrain that challenged my efforts and, sometimes, it was the emotions that the day brought with it. Eat, sleep, walk, repeat. Sounds doable. Averaging 25 km each and every day for a month straight while not only carrying a ten-to-twelve-pound daypack on my back but also weighted down with all the emotional baggage I brought along with me. The physical and mental obstacles I had to climb up and over each day. Eat, sleep, walk, repeat with shin splints, blisters, muscle aches and pains and an infected toe since day three. I keep saying this over and over again but I am seriously not ready for this to be over. If I had the ability, time and money to turn around and start this all over again, I would.

Oh, the joys of marriage. I can't begin to tell you how many times since Garry and I had that heartwarming and endearing conversation that we have had to revisit those areas of our relationship. It wasn't that long ago I brought up the fact that we once agreed we would work on finding balance between our work life and our home life. And, it wasn't that long ago that I reminded him how he said he was going to help out more around the house. Believe me, it's not because I am lazy. It's because there are certain tasks I seriously can't do anymore without suffering the painful consequences afterwards. And it wasn't that long ago that I explained how lonely I still feel in this relationship.

Is it time to look at this for what it is? Change only happens if you want it to. I want it to, but does he? Is he capable of change? Some people would flat out say that the answer would be a hard "No." Is it time for me to start asking myself the hard questions? I chuckle as I write that because I have already asked myself these questions over and over again. Can I accept him for who and how he is? Can I be content in this type of relationship? How much longer should I give him to prove that he is in this? I mean, he continues to say all the right things but actions, that's what it is about. Right?

There is still something there that keeps me here. When we spend time together doing things we both enjoy, we have a wonderful time, but those times are few and far between. He tries to convince me that when we go to the hardware store to pick out the materials we will use for the bathroom we are renovating is considered quality time together. That the drive we just took to Canadian Tire to grab some paint swatches is quality time together. I beg to differ. Yes, those are times spent together, but quality time? I see quality time as cuddling up on the couch without the distraction of Netflix or YouTube and having a genuine conversation, whether we are talking about special times we have shared together in the past, discussing our common goals for the future or just enjoying each other's company. Quality time, to me, is getting away from all the responsibilities we have here at home, parking the RV at our favorite lake, dropping the boat in the water and spending an hour or two trolling for fish. I don't need this "quality time" often but, when we only really see each other for maybe three hours a day during the week, it would be nice to make up for that lost time on the weekends.

It was actually quite sad revisiting this part of my journal. I knew that the conversation between Garry and I had to be done because my journey was coming to an end and I wanted to come home with all my cards on the table but the fact was, I still wasn't ready or really wanted to come home. I wasn't ready to stop walking. I wasn't done with "me" yet and there I was, still physically on "my" journey and I was jumping right back into "us". And also, as I revisit and read what was said and promised, I'm sad that after almost three years, little progress has been made. It hasn't all been bad, but it hasn't all been good either. Of course, there has been a lot of shit thrown at us in the past three years, but what is sad is that we are still re-visiting all the same broken promises that just continue to become re-broken broken promises. I can't continue to blame all the shit that has been thrown at us because, really, there is always going to be that shit being thrown. We should still be making the relationship our number one priority even while dodging or trudging through all that crap. Ugh, it makes my brain hurt.

The three things I am grateful for tonight are: That Garry didn't interrupt me when it was my turn to talk during the chat. I am grateful that I made, or took the first steps towards trusting him again and I am grateful that I am hopeful again.

CHAPTER 35
June 23, 2019: Pedrueza to Santiago de Compostela - 20 km

It is 10:30 pm and I am physically and emotionally exhausted. I am going to hold off until tomorrow to write as, for now, I just need to sleep.

I will say that I did walk into Santiago de Compostela with Helene and Gōran and before I could even accept the fact that I had actually just completed the Camino, I saw a girl run up to me with her arms wide open. It was Lisa, the girl I had walked with a few times during the last month. She had had issues with her knees so I would always slow my pace and keep her company. Unfortunately, there were a few sections where she had to take public transit but that's okay, she did it. There were a lot of people I recognized today, either because I had passed them along the Way or they had passed me, but I was so glad to see her and happy that she was able to complete her journey. We hugged for what seemed like forever.

That's all I wrote that day. I was thinking about editing this part so that it came off a little bit more exciting for the readers, if there are any, but then I thought "Nope." This is what I wrote and I am going to honor that.

CHAPTER 36
June 24, 2019: Santiago de Compostela

Again, I am going to wait until I am on the plane to Paris before writing about my last day on the Camino. I was going to take my journal to the square today and do some writing while I watched my fellow pilgrims make their arrivals but, the many times I was drawn to the square, all I wanted to do was "be" at the square. Nothing more. I wanted to sit and be and watch.

It's hard to explain but there is a kind of calming excitement that happens at the square and even though the pilgrims walking in have absolutely no idea that I am witnessing their last few steps on the Camino, I am almost positive they can feel my excitement, my joy and my appreciation of their hard work, dedication and effort. It doesn't matter where they started from, whether it was from Saint-Jean-Pied-de-Port, Sarria or from their own front door, they succeeded in what they came here to do. As I watch the tears, the laughter, the hugs and the celebrations, I almost feel the need to go over and thank them for allowing me to be a part of their special moment.

There were a lot of goodbyes today as everyone starts to make their way home. A few have decided to continue on to Finisterre or "The End of the World," something I now wish I had included but, maybe next time. For now, I just want to continue living in this moment.

The three things I am grateful for today — the wonderful experience the Camino provided me, the feeling of hope that I currently feel and I am grateful for the determination I have to bring this new person/new life back home to Canada

CHAPTER 37
June 25, 2019: Santiago de Compostela to Paris, France via Madrid

A twenty-minute taxi ride took me to the Santiago Airport and, as I gazed out the window at all the side streets and paths, I started to cry. Those are the routes I have grown accustomed to on the Camino and, so, that is where my eye is automatically drawn to. It didn't matter if there were several roads leading into a particular town, village or city; the yellow Camino arrows always seemed to point in the direction of the path less travelled. Seems weird to say that considering hundreds of thousands of people make it their goal to travel those "less travelled" paths or forgotten roads each and every year. Time and technology have created highways, pedestrian overpasses, underpasses and shortcuts, leaving those less known "yellow arrow marked" paths for the pilgrim.

I found myself looking for any sign of the Camino. A marker, an arrow or a weary pilgrim making their way into the city, but the farther away I got, the more disconnected I started to feel. It's all starting to feel like a distant memory and I am not even gone yet. I fear that all the hard work I put in these last thirty plus days will be lost. As I sit here at the airport, I swear most of the people here are fellow pilgrims. Some of them look vaguely familiar, but; the buffs and hats have been replaced with perfectly manicured hair. The disheveled hiking clothes have been converted into casual airport attire. This is all just a huge reminder that life continues on and I just have to stick with my resolve to take the Camino home with me rather than leave it here. Kelly reminded me last night that this has been my life for the last month or more and that now, I just have to make this my life – period.

Fast forward and I am now on my second, and shorter, flight from Madrid to Paris, France. Pilgrims have been replaced with young families who are obviously heading to Disneyland. There are way too many young girls wearing Mickey Mouse ears to think any different. By the time I land, I will no longer be in Spain, my home for the past month. The country that became my savior, teacher, guide – my heaven and my hell. I am feeling sad, scared, happy and anxious.

I am now prepared to write about:

June 23, 2019: Pedrueza to Santiago de Compostela 20 km and June 24, 2019: Free Day

I woke up the morning of June 23 and ran through the same routine I had been doing for the previous thirty-two days. Buckling up my daypack and tightening my sneakers, I left my pension and met Helene and Gōran at their albergue. Then, I proceeded to walk my final day on the Camino Frances.

Because of the directional error Helene and I made yesterday, the first few kilometers looked very familiar. Wrapped in a blanket of tall eucalyptus trees, I took a mental note to soak in every single moment of this day and not to rush things or wish certain parts of it away. It may sound weird but there have been times on this path where I have either wished that my immediate environment would just go away or that a specific day would just end. Like, when I would be in the middle of climbing a big hill and look up ahead just wishing I could trade places with the person I could see up at the top. I'm sure I am not the only one who has played that little game with themselves. But not today. Today, I wanted to feel it all, see it all and be a part of it all.

The three of us walked the entire day together. There were moments of talking and laughing followed by times of solitude and silence. There seemed to be this unspoken narrative that when one person fell behind it was for a reason and we respected that. Unless it was to stop and eat or take a collective break; when someone wanted to be alone, they were granted that wish.

The 20 km walk to Santiago de Compostela was a combination of gentle ascents to not so gentle ascents which were followed by a welcomed descent. It wouldn't be the Camino's style to give it up at the end and offer me a path that was on even ground the entire day. The first real village, Lavacolla, was 10 km from where I started this morning, followed by another 5 km before reaching Monte de Gozo, where we were given our first glimpse of the Promised Land off in the distance, just another 4 km away. Before I knew it, I was standing in front of a cement statue that read "Santiago." The first sign that we had reached the outskirts of the city, itself. Somewhere on the back of that monument, the three of us solidified our existence on the Camino by writing our names. The three Camino Amigos tattooed on this structure forever, or until the blue ink fades away with time and weather.

And, then just like that, I was standing in front of what resembled a large wire fence bearing the words "Santiago de Compostela." Attached to the wire fence; people had left behind various items as a token of their accomplishment. Walking sticks leaned up against it, buffs, hats, shirts, shoes and coats hung from it and all sorts of stickers had been placed on each individual letter. Even though we still had to walk into the city and find our way to the square, the day had gone by way too fast and I wasn't prepared for it to end. As much as I tried to slow down time and as hard as I attempted to focus all my effort into capturing every last detail of the day, it still got away from me.

We continued to follow the arrows, shells and various other markers that led us to the square. It wasn't until I heard the sound of distant bagpipes that I knew we were getting close. I had done enough research to know that there could possibly be a bagpipe player busking under the stone archway leading to the finish line. Knowing that I was getting close, I got out my phone and started recording.

I walked into the square of Santiago de Compostela with Helene and Gōran and, although we walked through the archway together, it felt like the moment we came out on the other side, we were instantly separated. It wasn't like we lost sight of each other or started walking in separate directions because we were still very much standing beside each other. Maybe it was because we were all, individually, feeling our own feelings and attempting to process everything in our own minds. To me, it felt like I had been picked up by a tornado and everything and everyone were spinning and moving around at warp speed. The square is huge and the Cathedral is enormous and mesmerizing. There were pilgrims laughing, clapping, taking pictures, standing, sitting, jumping for joy and running to people they recognized. Like I said earlier, I was immediately embraced by a girl I had walked with along the Way, which kind of snapped me out of my daze. Like waking from a dream, the three of us, once again, came together and celebrated our extraordinary accomplishment together.

Just like every other person who had done what we had just done, we took the obligatory pictures marking our extraordinary accomplishments. Of course, with the Cathedral acting as our backdrop, we took one of the three of us together followed by individual ones as well. I even took a picture of my colorfully painful big toe nail as it proudly posed in front of this beautiful building that represents the burial place of Saint James, himself.

Then, we just sat down.

We found a place and just sat.

It was such a weird moment. I knew I was there and I knew it was over but it just wasn't resonating, so, I just continued to sit there looking up at the spectacular building that this city was literally built around. It's hard to explain, but the air seemed to be filled with the excitement, relief, angst and joy of everyone in the square and, at times, I felt like I was intruding on someone else's moment. But then, we were all a part of each other's individual moments because we had all shared the journey it took to get here. And, I am not even talking about the Camino Frances. There are seven or eight well established routes and even then, you can mix and match them up. It didn't matter what specific route your journey took you on, it's about the physical, emotional, mental and spiritual journey we had all just gone through. Every single person there was experiencing, in their own way, the same thing that the person beside them, in front of them and even behind them was experiencing. It was like we were all together but in separate groups, even those who were sitting silently alone. We were all sharing this very specific bond that was now tying us all together. I have written this before, but we were a family – a Camino family.

After soaking in the reality of our surroundings, we parted ways, but not before making arrangements to meet back at the square later to partake in a celebratory drink. Gōran went to find a place to stay and Helene and I went to get our Compostela, our official Camino Certificate to prove that we just did what we just did. Doing that served as yet another reminder that this part of my journey was over.

No matter how hard I tried to avoid it, everything continued to happen at warp speed and I believe it was due in part to the excitement and energy emanating off of everyone. Although the line up at the Pilgrim's Office was long, it felt as if it took mere seconds before I was the one at the head of it. In a blink of an eye, I was standing at the counter in front of the person who would put the final stamp in my Pilgrim Credential and also, the one who would place my name on the Compostela as proof of my pilgrimage. And, as quickly as that task was done, I was off to find my hotel to check that off the list as well.

While preparing for this journey, it was suggested that, as a celebratory gesture to myself, I splurge and book my two nights in Santiago de Compostela at a higher ranked hotel. The Hotel Monumento San Francisco would be my home for the remainder of my time in Spain. Rated as a 4-star hotel, it was originally a huge historical monastery located in a great location and less than five hundred feet from the Cathedral. Although it was equipped with a pool and a hot tub, I didn't use either during my stay. The room was very spacious and elegant but, for the amount of time I actually spent there, I felt like it was a bit unnecessary.

Although the location was ideal, had I known what my accommodations would be like along the Camino, I would have just stuck with a 1–2-star hotel in Santiago de Compostela. I didn't realize that the rating system in Spain was, obviously, a lot different than what I am used to. What they consider to be a 1-star room would be considered a solid 3 for me, personally. Sure, some of the rooms were small and others had the bare minimum of what I had requested, but I was fortunate enough to have those little splurges along the Way without even knowing it. This was because I chose not to know what my room was going to look like ahead of time so I never looked them up online before I left for Spain. Those times I walked into a room and saw a bathtub instead of a shower was an unexpected treat and that one night I basically had a fully furnished apartment all to myself was amazing. So, by the time I arrived in Santiago de Compostela, I didn't feel like I needed that little extra comfort. Just a note to self.

After getting cleaned up, I met Gōran and Helene for drinks and even then, it felt a little chaotic. At some point during my absence, it was decided that a group of people, including Helene, who had walked together pretty much from the beginning would gather together in the square to take a group photograph. A photo that I was invited to be a part of but declined because, besides Helene, Gōran and Mary, I hadn't really walked with any of the others so, I volunteered to be the cameraperson. It wasn't until we actually stepped into the square to take the picture that the chaos stopped. It was just such a magical place. Again, with the Cathedral in the background and a bunch of cell phones and cameras at my feet waiting for their turn to capture the perfect shot, I snapped photo after photo until everyone in the group was satisfied. Once the cameras and cell phones had been retrieved and the group dissipated, I looked around at my surroundings and then, once again, I just sat.

It's hard to explain the impulse that washes over you when you are standing in the square. The impulse to choose the spot you are currently standing in and just sit down. The Cathedral Square in Santiago de Compostela has that effect on you. Filled with energy, excitement, achievement, joy, love and gratitude, it literally welcomes you to pop a squat, as the kids say. It invites you to just "watch" and to just "be" and so, I did. I did that on several occasions. As the day went on, I continued to see people I knew and I rejoiced in their success as they did me. As exhausted as I was, I didn't want any of it to end. Even after saying goodnight to my friends, I stayed behind and tried to capture as much as I could before finally making my way back to my hotel. Turning my light out at 2:30 am, exhausted by the emotional blur of a day I had just lived, I literally shook my head at how quickly not only this day had gone by, but also the last thirty-two.

I woke up the morning of June 24 and said goodbye to my walking stick like I was never going to see it again. Filled with emotion, I reluctantly handed it over to the gentleman at the Oficina Postal who then took full responsibility for what, I felt, had been my life line during some of the most difficult stages of the Camino, both physically and emotionally. That was a lot of responsibility he was holding in his hand. I had held on to that walking stick for six to nine hours a day for the last month so, sending it off by mail was like chopping off my arm and mailing it home with the hope that it would actually make it there in one piece. But, taking a look around and seeing boxes of all shapes and sizes and noticing that they ship just about anything to anywhere, I knew my stick would be in good hands. I mean, if they can mail somebody's bike back home for them – they can ship my stick.

It was my free day in Santiago. Gōran had already started his journey back to Sweden and Helene, who had actually arrived in Santiago earlier than expected, was considering moving her flight up by a few days. But for today, we still had each other so we shopped and ate and sat. We also did something that is considered to be the ultimate tradition, ritual, custom or whatever you want to call it. We stood in line and waited for our turn to walk up a few stairs and embrace Saint James the Apostle.

At the back of the main altar is a large figure of Saint James and, because there was a large amount of construction going on, I'm pretty sure the way we had to go about doing it really wasn't the normal way, but, after maneuvering through a really unorganized line, we, one at a time, walked up a couple of stairs, stood behind the statue and again, from behind, hugged the statue of Saint James while offering our thanks for helping us get here. I'm not religious but I am spiritual, so I was sincere in my thanks and hoped my words reached the ears they needed to reach. We then went beneath the Main Altar and tried to visit the Tomb of St. James whose remains are said to be kept in a silver urn I briefly got to see. Unfortunately, there were two men kneeling in front of it when I walked through who had no intentions of getting up and who seemed to not notice the large amount of people starting to congregate behind them. The small space was getting very crowded to the point where we were actually getting pushed out before I could snap a good picture.

When Helene was done for the day, we hugged one final time and I returned to the square to, once again, sit. As I watched more pilgrims come in and perform the same rituals I had done yesterday, a sense of sadness came over me. Now what? I allowed my mind to contemplate that for a moment and then I was brought back into the "now" by a familiar face or two. I saw many people during my long walk across Northern Spain and when joint recognition was established in the square, there would be hugs and smiles and words of congratulations. I would offer to take their picture and then they would be off to the next person they recognized.

As much as I attempted to slow the clock, time just wouldn't stop. Knowing I had an early wake-up call, I tore myself away from Cathedral Square for the last time and went back to my hotel room to pack. There were so many items I had depended and relied on the last thirty-two days that were just no longer relevant, so I left them behind. Their spot in my suitcase was quickly replaced by trinkets and souvenirs I had purchased during the day.

Which leads me back to today, June 25th. I went from Santiago de Compostela to Madrid and, from Madrid, caught this current flight to Paris. I am thirty-five minutes out from landing in Paris' Orly Airport. I had previously landed in Charles de Gaulle Airport so I have absolutely no idea how I will be getting to my hotel when I land but I am also not worried about it. I Will Find My Way.

EPILOGUE

June 25, 2019

I did arrive safely at my hotel in Paris. I decided to stay at the Hotel Moulin Vert for both my pre and post Camino. It is a small but quaint hotel situated on a quiet street in a very ideal location close to the Metro Stations I will be using to sightsee. The room is small but there is only one of me and I really don't need a lot of space. Taking the bus from the airport and then walking from the Gare Montparnasse to my hotel; I checked in at approximately 3:45 pm and then immediately turned around and started making my way to the Eiffel Tower. I really only have the remainder of today and all of tomorrow in Paris, so I am going to see as much of it as possible. Europe is having a massive heat wave, so the city is offering free Metro to ease the torture of standing in a crowded sardine can with temperatures of up to 36° Celsius.

The Eiffel Tower is pretty impressive. I took the mandatory pictures from right underneath it but that was about it. I had no desire to spend the money to go to the top. It was also pretty crowded so, as much as I wanted to see it, I was also content with not sticking around the area for too long. There were a couple of other interesting things around so I moved on.

I visited the Musee de l'Armee which was huge and a lot less crowded but just as impressive. The dome of this building is said to hold the tomb of Napoleon. I then walked to the Pont Alexandre III Bridge, Paris' deck arch bridge that spans the Seine River and is noted as the most ornate and extravagant bridge in the city. As much as I tried to enjoy the moment as well as the architecture of this beautiful bridge, it just made me think of all the bridges I had crossed on the Camino.

Bridges that made me verbally gasp or dramatically shake my head in disbelief. Those bridges made me feel something. With those bridges, I was in awe of the fact that I was actually in the presence of something brilliant and historic. I also feel like I am experiencing a huge culture shock while still trying to enjoy my time in Paris. I mean, I am in Paris, France and yet I am literally nine hundred and thirty miles away.

June 26, 2019

Today started bright and early. I had pre-purchased my ticket to the Louvre so that I could go and see the famous Mona Lisa and, when doing so, I had to choose a time of arrival and I chose 11:00 am. What a disappointment she was and I'm an art lover. I actually graduated high school on the Honor Roll for the Arts. The Louvre holds some of the most beautiful pieces of art I have ever seen but I literally had to look up to see them because some of the most impressive ones were displayed on the ceiling. I finally worked my way to the room where the Mona Lisa was being held. And it was work. The map I was given led me in one direction but, apparently, they had recently moved her. I then enlisted the help of one of their employees who pointed me in the right direction. I walked into a brilliantly white walled room with a large group of people gathered at the far end of it. Instinctively, I joined in and made my way closer to the front of the crowd to gaze upon the famous Mona Lisa – a painting the size of a postage stamp. Really? I took the picture, stared at her for a moment and then walked out. The room that immediately followed had dark burgundy walls lined with the largest paintings I have ever seen. The whole room was adorned with the most intricate, vibrant and amazing pieces and, just like that, my moment with the Mona Lisa was instantly forgotten.

I visited several exhibits before deciding to take a break. I purchased a Coke Zero and a cookie and sat down for a bit of a rest. Looking over some of the literature I had received upon my arrival, I noticed that the Venus de Milo was actually being stored at the Louvre and, although, I had full intentions of leaving after my snack, I knew I was probably never going to be here again so I had to go and see her. I know I make it sound like a chore, but the Louvre is huge and, of course, the Venus de Milo was not in an area that was anywhere close to me. Finishing up, I went on the hunt for the famous statue of Aphrodite and I was not disappointed. She was stunning. Another picture to commemorate the moment.

One of the metros on my route was situated inside a shopping mall so, while I was in there, I decided to walk around. It soon became apparent that there were just way too many people and way too much noise. Too much, too soon. I haven't been in very many "crowds" in the last month and it was extremely overwhelming. My next thought was to head to the Notre Dame district, grab a gelato and do some people watching but, there again, I was starting to feel a little overwhelmed. There were just too many people and too much noise.

I headed back to my hotel for a bathroom break because there are literally no bathrooms anywhere in Paris, even when you follow signs falsely leading you to an area that's supposed to have bathroom facilities. I also had to fill up my water bottle in hopes that it would help beat the heat.

While taking in the solitude and silence of my hotel room, I decided I would venture back to my favorite part of the city which is by the Pont Alexandre III Bridge. Reason being is that it doesn't give off a "touristy" vibe, it is a wide-open and non-congested area with a nice park to sit in and some beautiful older buildings to look at. Doesn't matter where you go in Paris, there is art everywhere and this extravagant bridge is just one more example of it, as four huge bronze sculptures of winged horses stand proudly on top of it while connecting one district to another.

I ate my last Paris meal in my small hotel room. A chicken and tomato croissant made up of individual ingredients I had picked up at a nearby grocery store and concocted on my own. Then, out of some sort of obligation, I walked around the block and tried to absorb every ounce of Europe I could before I leave. Coming back to my room for the final time, I have to admit that I really don't want to be here. I am not going to say that I regret my decision to end my Camino with an extra day in Paris, I created this specific Itinerary without knowing how I would feel or how I would be at the end of my long walk. But now, I feel totally out of place and overwhelmed. I, again, describe it as a culture shock. There is just too much noise, too many cars and way too many people. Knowing now what I didn't' know in the planning stage, I would have preferred to carry on from Santiago de Compostela and walked to Finisterre and Muxia. At least in Finisterre, I would have still been surrounded by people in the same mindset as me. I want to believe that it would have been a bit more of an intimate and quieter experience and a more subtle shift back to reality rather than a hard push. Instead, I went and threw myself right back into the thick of things and I am just not prepared for it. I am extremely grateful that I got to see Paris and experience some of the same things that Ken did when he was here. I am just not ready to let go of the Camino and, by being here, it feels as if it is already gone.

As much as I am looking forward to getting home to Garry, my cats and then, eventually, the rest of the family, I am still craving, and needing peace, quiet, simplicity and time to reflect – if that makes sense at all. Having just experienced the last day and a half here in Paris, I am now realizing how hard it is going to be to not fall back into the routine of life back home. The peace and quiet of the Camino made it easier to ponder these things where as the noise and congestion of Paris has totally drowned those thoughts out. I am afraid that my life back home will have the same effect. I just have to remember that I was not happy and it was not healthy. I want a simple, stress free, joyful and humble existence. I want to be happy.

June 27, 2019

Today was filled with metros, trains and planes. I began the day maneuvering around two metro lines to the train that would then take me to Charles de Gaulle Airport. I arrived at Charles de Gaulle only to be greeted by a very crowded, hectic and frustrating airport containing huge lines of extremely cranky people who all felt as if their needs were way more important than mine (and everyone else's). The seven-and-a-half-hour flight from Paris to Montreal was just okay. I watched a couple of complimentary movies, got fed and listened to a bunch of crying children, one of whom decided it would be entertaining to kick my chair for hours on end. I arrived in Montreal to more crowds, luggage issues and two trips through security because of the water bottle Kelly had given me for this trip. Apparently, the water that was allowed on the previous flight was no longer allowed on this flight so, instead of just letting me drink the remainder of the water, I had to turn around and go through the whole routine all over again. I got to the gate just as they were starting to board, giving me no time whatsoever to calm down from the whole security fiasco. As I write this, I am now on a five-and-a-half-hour flight to Vancouver that promises to be bumpy the whole way.

Doing the math, it is now technically midnight "my time" or the time I have acclimated to, it's really only 6:00 pm Montreal time and even earlier back home in British Columbia. I know I need to get some rest; however, it is hard to think about sleep when I look out the window and see nothing but clear blue skies. I yearn and, yes, I said yearn, for some quiet. I ache to be back in Spain and not just back in Spain, but back on the Camino where there is a constant sense of calm instead of the hustle and bustle I have surrounded myself with today. Maybe this is still the Camino testing my resolve and, boy, has it been tested.

The Camino Frances may be many miles away but it is now embedded in my soul and I need to hold on to that, tightly if need be. I need to try and live the life the Camino has provided me this past month. I have to remember all I learned along the Way and go after the things I want and deserve. I want less chaos and less stress and I want more peace and serenity. I don't think that is too much to ask for.

The farther away I get from Europe the sadder I feel. Not for Paris, but for the "Way." I miss the people I met, the places I walked through and the feeling of calm I found. I am not feeling all that calm right now. I miss the simplicity of getting up each morning and just walking. Don't get me wrong, it was physically, emotionally and mentally draining, but there was always a feeling of joy, peace and happiness and I am just so scared I will lose that in my everyday life. I am so grateful for the Camino and all the gifts it gave me. I want more!

From Vancouver, I will take one more short flight to Kelowna which will be followed by a two-hour car ride home. Garry will be picking me up at the airport and then, together, we will figure out where we go from there. Hopefully, our path will continue being one spent together on but, if not, then my journey will continue. And if that has to be done alone then I will have to be okay with that. I need to start making my needs my priority. So, for the last time in this journal I will note what I am grateful for. Today, I am grateful for MY courage, MY strength and MY abilities. Yes, today is all about me.

WHAT I PACKED FOR THE CAMINO FRANCES

CLOTHING:

Poncho x 1 – Cheap one	Used maybe 4 or 5 times.
Rain Pants x 1	Wore twice, left behind early on.
Lightweight Gore-Text Jacket x 1	
Pair of Gloves x 1	Always in my jacket pocket. Wore a few times.
Fleece Pullover x 1	
Solomon Women's Speed Cross 4 Trail Running Shoes x 1	Make it a size larger than you normally wear. I didn't and paid for it with an infected toe.
Chaco Hiking Sandals x 1	
Flip Flops x 1 – Cheap pair	Maybe used them twice.
Buff x 2	
Marino Wool Light Weight Ankle Socks x 3	
Sports Bra x 1	
Moisture Wicking Panties x 3	
Marino Wool T-Shirt x 2	
Long Sleeve Synthetic Shirt x 1	
Tank Top x 1	
SweetLegs x 1 (pair of tights)	
Shorts x 1	
Hiking Skort x 1	Wore it once, left behind early on.
Hanes Thermal Long Underwear Set x 1 (long sleeve shirt and pants)	Didn't wear the shirt much but did wear the thermal pants as actual PANTS every day on the trail.
PJ's x 1	Consisted of a t-shirt and boy shorts.
Sunglasses x 1 pair	

TOILETRIES:

Toothbrush, toothpaste and Floss	Travel size.
Anti-Perspirant	
Small Hair Gel	
Travel Size Hairspray	
SPF Lip Chapstick	
Small Jar of Vaseline	To put on my feet in the morning.
Travel Size Sunscreen	
Travel Sewing Kit	Scissors, needles, thread, safety pins.
First Aid Kit	Lighter, band aids, Polysporin, antiseptic pads, Aleve, anti-inflammatory and pain medication, Imodium, jack knife, mole skin for blisters, nail clippers and tweezers.
Small Hand Sanitizer	
Ear Plugs	Couple of the cheap packs.

GEAR:

Osprey Daylite Daypack	13 Litre.
Small Carry-on Suitcase	
Walking Stick from Home	I had to check it as oversized luggage but it was worth it though.
Water Bottle from Home	
Money Belt	
Fanny Pack	Yup – and I would do it again.
Head Lamp	Never used it once.
Camino de Santiago Guidebook	By Sergi Ramis.
Camino Passport	Credential for Stamps.

EXTRAS:

Soap Leaves	Disposable laundry soap sheets. (container of 50)
Clip Hooks x 2	Which I hung from my daypack.
Large Freezer Bags x 2	One was used for my electronics.
Small Ziplock Bags x 4	One was used for random extras.
Couple of Twist Ties and Elastic Bands	
Hydralyte Packages x 8	Used once but they are really good to have.
Book x 1	True Crime. Can't sleep without reading for a bit.
Journal x 1	
Rock from Home	I packed Coral

ELECTRONICS:

European Travel Plug Adapter x 2	I forgot one at a hostel so I was glad I had the extra one.
Phone from Home	
Phone Charger x 1	
Headphones x 1	Used twice and then I lost them.
Power Bank x 1	Didn't use it at all.

ESSENTIALS:

Passport	
Driver's License	
All Medical Cards	eg: extended medical information.
Visa and Debit Card	
Travel Insurance Documentation	
Copies of Driver's License and Passport	I kept these separate from the real things.
Money	
All Itineraries and Tickets	Airline and train etc.

BIBLIOGRAPHY

Ramis, S. (2014, 2017) *Camino de Santiago.* London, EN: Aurum Press
Your Way Adventures (2019) *Camino de Santiago Guidebook. Trail
Guide Camino Frances St-Jean-Pied-de-Port to Santiago de
Compostela.* Your Way Adventures

Printed in Great Britain
by Amazon

33406785R00154